DANIEL DENNETT

The Continuum Contemporary American Thinkers series offers concise and accessible introductions to the most important and influential thinkers at work in philosophy today. Designed specifically to meet the needs of students and readers encountering these thinkers for the first time, these informative books provide a coherent overview and analysis of each thinker's vital contribution to the field of philosophy. The series is the ideal companion to the study of these most inspiring and challenging of thinkers.

Continuum Contemporary American Thinkers:
Saul Kripke, Arif Ahmed
Hilary Putnam, Lance P. Hickey

Forthcoming:
John Searle, Joshua Rust

DANIEL DENNETT

DAVID L. THOMPSON

continuum

Continuum International Publishing Group

The Tower Building	80 Maiden Lane
11 York Road	Suite 704
London SE1 7NX	New York NY 10038

www.continuumbooks.com

British Library Cataloguing-in-Publication Data
A catalogue record for this book is available from the British Library.

ISBN: HB: 978-1-8470-6007-5
PB: 978-1-8470-6008-2

Library of Congress Cataloging-in-Publication Data
Thompson, David, 1941-
Daniel Dennett / David Thompson.
p. cm.
ISBN 978-1-84706-007-5–ISBN 978-1-84706-008-2
1. Dennett, Daniel Clement. I. Title.
B945.D394T46 2009
191—dc22

2008051183

Typeset by Newgen Imaging Systems Pvt Ltd, Chennai, India
Printed and bound in Great Britain by the
MPG Books Group

CONTENTS

PREFACE

Daniel Dennett is one of the foremost contemporary philosophers. His work synthesizes traditional philosophical themes—mind, self, freedom, ethics—with current scientific theories. His aim is positive: he thinks we can have our cake and eat it too. We can accept the view science gives us of the world and still maintain human dignity and value. More than that: Dennett argues that science offers us a better foundation for the things we hold dear than traditional philosophical, religious, or commonsensical accounts ever could.

This book is an introduction and does not presuppose prior familiarity with Dennett's philosophy. My aim is to explain some of Dennett's central positions and his reasons for them. Since Dennett's output is enormous, a book of this length cannot hope to do justice to all his ideas, detailed arguments, and fascinating thought-experiments. My hope is that it may inspire readers to examine Dennett's own original writings. Happily, this is not an onerous task, for he writes in a clear and invigorating style and frequently addresses those who are not experts in philosophy or science.

Since I think Dennett's ideas are radical, I try to place his arguments in the wider context of Western philosophy, particularly of Modern philosophy since Descartes. The significance of his solutions can best be understood if we grasp the perplexities that have tied earlier philosophers in knots.

Dennett's solutions are controversial, so there is a large secondary literature of criticism and commentary. For the most part, I will be referring to these controversies only when they will help us to clarify some of Dennett's own positions. My preference is to present our author through his own lights rather than through the criticisms and interpretations—often misinterpretations—of commentators.

This is not to claim that my own exposition is utterly objective. While I do my best to present Dennett's ideas faithfully, my philosophical formation has given me my own criteria for determining which issues are important, which contrasts are worth making, and which arguments are to be emphasized. The very act of selecting from Dennett's thousands of pages the few central themes that can be covered in a short book involves judgements about their relative importance and interest. This book is, necessarily, an *interpretation*.

My understanding of Dennett has developed slowly over three decades as I discussed his ideas during courses, seminars, and conferences. I am grateful to students at Memorial University of Newfoundland, McGill University, University College Dublin, and Victoria University of Wellington, who have challenged me as I grappled with Dennett's thought. The sharp criticisms of my philosophy colleagues at Memorial University have been especially helpful in forcing me to clarify his arguments.

I thank particularly my colleague Evan Simpson who graciously undertook to read the entire manuscript and whose comments have greatly improved it.

Thanks are also due to Sarah Campbell who first invited me to write this book, to Heather Myers who encouraged me, and to Tom Crick who has guided me through the process.

Above all, I want to thank Dan Dennett himself, not only for his creative ideas, but also for his concern to communicate these ideas with patience and gentle perseverance to those who, like myself, have been initially slow to grasp their significance.

ABBREVIATIONS

Key books and papers by Dennett are referred to by letter codes as follows. Detailed bibliographical information can be found in the bibliography.

BC   *Brainchildren: Essays on Designing Minds.* 1998
BS   *Breaking the Spell.* 2006
CC   *Content and Consciousness.* 1969
CE   *Consciousness Explained.* 1991
CNG   "The self as a center of narrative gravity." 1986
DC   *Dennett and His Critics.* 1993
DDI   *Darwin's Dangerous Idea: Evolution and the Meanings of Life.* 1995
DP   "With a little help from my friends," in *Dennett's Philosophy.* 2000
EE   "The evolution of evaluators." 1997
ER   *Elbow Room: The Varieties of Free Will Worth Wanting.* 1984
FE   *Freedom Evolves.* 2003
IS   *The Intentional Stance.* 1987
PHD   "How to protect human dignity from science." 2008
QQ   "Quining Qualia." 1988
SD   *Sweet Dreams.* 2005

CHAPTER 1

THE PROJECT OF NATURALISM

What is consciousness? How could a brain state be conscious? How can neurons be about objects? Could a computer be conscious of objects in its world? Since brains are neural computers, do we not already have computers with intentionality?

I am concerned about myself, my actions in the past, my current experience, and the destiny of my "self" in the future. Yet is this not all an illusion? From a scientific point of view, must we not say that there are no "selves"? How can we reconcile science with the existence of humans who hold ethical, political, aesthetic, and religious values?

The scientific world appears to be value-free. The human world is imbued with values. From a humanistic point of view, it is love and hate, peace and violence, and the good and the bad that give meaning to our lives. Do these human characteristics have any place in a scientific approach to the world?

If we apply science to human beings, must we not assume that human actions are all determined by causal laws and so we can never act freely? Is the free will that we hold so dear a chimera that we must renounce if we are to accept the scientific worldview?

Are we faced with a stark choice: either renounce our humanistic view of the world or reject the vision of science as the project of universal explanation?

These are the kinds of questions that Daniel Dennett grapples with.

DANIEL DENNETT

Daniel C. Dennett (b. 1942) is one of the most popular and influential of contemporary American philosophers. While he is primarily identified with the Anglo-American, analytic school of philosophy, a number of his central themes would be congenial to phenomenological and continental thinkers. Dennett studied philosophy at Harvard University, where he was a student of W. V. O. Quine. While at Harvard, he reports being significantly influenced by Husserlian phenomenology. He did his doctorate at Oxford University under the mentorship of Gilbert Ryle, a thinker whose behaviorist criticisms of Cartesian dualism permeate Dennett's discussions of consciousness. Dennett initially established his reputation in the philosophy of mind (*Content and Consciousness*, *The Intentional Stance*, *Consciousness Explained*) but has since written widely on ontology, cognitive science, robotics, freedom, Darwinian evolution, ethics, religion, and other areas. Disparate as these writings might seem at first sight, they are unified by one overarching vision that aims to synthesize human experience with the scientific worldview.

HISTORICAL CONTEXT OF NATURALISM

To understand Dennett's thought we need to place it in its historical context of Western philosophy. The development of modern science in the 16th century threw philosophical thought into a quandary. The new sciences were founded on the principles of mechanism: all effects are explained by causes; causes obey natural, deterministic laws; nature is an objective realm independent of observers; and value and purpose are to be exiled from the natural order. The role of language is to describe and explain the world, not to construct it or to influence it by magical incantations. In contrast to the objective reality of nature, human experience is relegated to the realm of subjective appearance.

Mechanism leaves little room for the human world. Some, e.g., Thomas Hobbes, bit the bullet and proposed that natural scientific methodology be applied to all phenomena including the human. Initially this was primarily a dogmatic position, but as the centuries passed and empirical method was applied to human activities by the social and psychological sciences, ideology gave way to a vision supported by substantial application of reason to society, values, and mind. Materialists suggested that humanistic phenomena are illusions generated by primitive mythologies, destined to be reduced by developing theories of the natural order and ultimately eliminated. The scientific worldview would then be completely victorious, defeat the humanistic view of the world and show that freedom, morality, beauty, and love are illusions. A materialistic vision of this nature can be called eliminativist.

The only alternative to eliminativism appeared to be dualism. Dualism grants that there is a natural order, the order of matter, about which scientific knowledge rules supreme; but it maintains that there is also a second order of reality, mind, that can act as a refuge for all those humanistic phenomena exiled from nature by science. In the order of mind, reason replaces cause, freedom trumps determinism, and purpose and value overcome blind natural laws. By declaring that mind and matter are two independent substances that have no properties in common, dualism allows science to progress without interference from subjective, religious, or other human interests; at the same time, it protects from encroachments by science the values, gods, and social relationships that make life worth living.

This line in the sand drawn by dualists has been challenged from the very beginning, but recent scientific developments have made the isolation of the mind less and less plausible: the social sciences discovered causal regularities in society; Darwin integrated the human into the biological; and recent advances in brain science have revealed that cognition, emotion, and action are founded on neurophysiological processes. The weaknesses of dualism appear to leave eliminativist materialism, apparently the only alternative, the victor.

Dennett does not believe that these two alternatives are incompatible. The essence of his approach is to grant the validity of humanistic phenomena yet integrate them into the scientific worldview. Unlike the eliminative position, he grants the reality of consciousness, freedom, morality, and so on; but he differentiates his view from dualism by claiming that mental and human phenomena can be explained by the scientific method. This approach requires certain compromises. Some humanistic characteristics need to be deflated to reflect what they really are in our experience, as opposed to various inflated, metaphysical, or absolutist interpretations of them. Not every philosophical or theoretical conception of freedom or of consciousness can be preserved, but the essential features of them—what we really want—can be. On the other hand, certain adjustments or concessions need to be made on the scientific side. The scientific method will need to be stretched in a number of ways: the study of the brain will need to include functional and intentional analyses; it must adopt heterophenomenological methods; and Darwinian evolutionary theory will need to be expanded to include the theory of memes: memetics. (I will explain these concepts later.)

This compromise position can be called naturalism. A full account of Dennett's project of naturalism is the subject matter of the rest of this book, so at this point I will deal only with some general, overall features of the position. First of all, to explain something naturalistically is to show how it fits into nature. The most obvious alternative to explaining things in terms of nature is to explain them by what is outside nature: by the supernatural. Appealing to gods, to spirits, or to other forces beyond nature is what naturalism primarily opposes. To explain the devastation of a hurricane by appealing to the arbitrary anger of the gods would be a typical supernaturalist explanation. Nature, in contrast, is a realm governed by laws that are regular and impersonal. The naturalist project is the attempt to explain all phenomena by appeal to such natural processes.

The mechanism of Thomas Hobbes or Baron d'Holbach understands nature only as physical nature, and so holds that all explanation must be in terms of universal physical laws. Dennett, however, has a more inclusive notion of nature that includes regularities that emerge as a result of biological evolutionary processes. The regularities that govern biological organisms and systems are of a functional nature based on evolutionary adaptation and, while they do not violate any universal physical laws, they offer a mode of explanation that goes beyond the purely physical while remaining naturalistic. For example, many organisms have evolved behaviors that respond to light, but an explanation of these responses solely in terms of optics or light quanta would be inadequate. We can only understand these behaviors if we take into account the functions that they play in predation, in defence, in mating, and so on, and grasp the evolutionary history that led to their emergence. To explain human phenomena in terms of biology or functional neurophysiology is still, as Dennett understands it, naturalism.

In a more controversial move, Dennett holds that Darwinian adaptationism also applies to cultural traits. In the human cultural and linguistic environment, some traits adapt better than others and so survive while others die out. Treating murder as a crime is a trait that has replicated widely because of its superior adaptive

4

features in human cultures. This kind of explanation of the crim-
inality of murder—as opposed, for example, to appeal to a divine
commandment—still counts as a naturalistic explanation, according to Dennett.

The project of naturalism, then, goes beyond what is purely physical or mechanistic. The "nature" that Dennett appeals to is more
than mechanism, but it falls far short of anything "supernatural."

DENNETT AND CONTEMPORARY THOUGHT

In contemporary thought, Dennett's philosophy of mind grows
out of functionalism. Functionalism identifies mental states by the
role they play in the mind or the brain. It is opposed, on the one
hand, to dualist claims that mental states cannot be explained in
terms of brain processes. John Searle and Colin McGinn defend
dualist positions something like this. On the other hand, functionalism also rejects physicalism, that is, the claim that mental states
are defined by the material substrate of which they are composed.
Functionalists hold that mental functions are multiply realizable:
two mental states are identical if they fulfill the same psychological
function even if the neural processes that instantiate them are quite
different. Physicalism leads to eliminative materialism, that is, to
the claim that describing human experience and behavior by means
of mental predicates can, at least in some distant future theory, be
abandoned in favor of descriptions couched only in physical and
neurological terms. Patricia and Paul Churchland are examples of
contemporary philosophers who defend the eliminativist position.

Functionalists, such as Hilary Putnam (in his early work), position themselves between these two extremes. Mental states are
not mysteries beyond the reach of science; nevertheless, we cannot eliminate reference to them by appealing to purely physical
categories. While Dennett also positions himself between two
extremes, his position is more sophisticated than traditional functionalism. The traditional position considers mental states as real
states of the brain, albeit functional states. Dennett denies that
mental states are real in the sense of being things-in-themselves (I
adopt the term based on Kant's *Ding-an-sich*). Dennett holds that
mental states are attributed to an organism from within a specific
point of view, from a stance, as he puts it. His position is clearly
influenced by the philosophical behaviorism of Gilbert Ryle and

the later Wittgenstein. (Dennett's theory of stances will be a major concern of Chapter 6.)

In his philosophy of mind, then, Dennett eschews the traditional dichotomies and moves toward a carefully nuanced, third alternative. The same spirit imbues his philosophy as a whole. When he moves on from consciousness to consider selfhood, freedom, and ethics, he invariably transcends the usual dualist/physicalist standoffs and offers approaches that criticize the common presuppositions shared by both camps. Typically, instead of looking at phenomena as they currently exist, he investigates how they came to be. He relies on a Darwinian, evolutionary perspective that allows us to see how we can get from a world without freedom, selfhood, or whatever, to our own world, where they are present. The way from there to here involves gradual steps; hence there are intermediate phenomena that don't fit neatly into our current categories. These steps, however, are not purely biological: Dennett extends Darwinian adaptationism beyond genes to include cultural traits—"memes"— that permit humans to escape the confines of the purely biological. This gradualist, stepwise development means we should expect to find intermediate stages that are hard to categorize: self-like characteristics in entities that are not yet human selves; processes that are on the way to free will, but not there yet; and values that, while not based on pure selfishness, are not yet truly ethical ones. It is in this history, full of ambiguities, that Dennett finds the origins, and therefore the present nature, of mind and humanistic values.

In each of the following chapters I will be concerned not only to discuss Dennett's views on the chapter's topic, but I will also be showing how his approach to each of these issues is founded in his overall project of naturalism. The chapters cover a wide gamut of topics: consciousness, freedom, selfhood, evolution, ontology, ethics, and religion. These are not issues chosen at random. Behind the approach to each of these topics is a unifying vision of how humans and their lives can be integrated into the scientific worldview without undermining their importance, validity, and value. Whether he is talking about the relationship between consciousness and neurons, between physical determinism and freedom, or between evolutionary processes and social values, in every case Dennett opposes those who would either undermine or eliminate human values in the name of science, or would dispute and limit the scientific worldview by putting the human in some way beyond the scientific account. He wants it both ways: the human and the scientific are not only compatible; they support each other.

Given this project, it is to be expected that Dennett's writings have a multidisciplinary flavor. Since his aim is to relate the human to the brain, to evolution and cultural history and to the natural world in general, it is inevitable that he has to discuss material in neurophysiology, biology, and history—material often avoided by philosophers. But Dennett is not a philosopher's philosopher. Apart from his interdisciplinarity, he is committed to getting the message out beyond academia. To a considerable extent, his writings are directed, beyond professional philosophy, to the thinking population in general, the intelligentsia of our age, who Dennett thinks are blocked in their ideas by the simplistic standoff between the two solitudes, between science and humanism. Humanists should embrace science; science should apply its methods to humanistic issues. Philosophers, perhaps, should lead the way in overcoming this blockage, but largely because philosophers are the source of the obstacle in the first place. The task of creating a synthetic worldview is not for philosophers alone; it is a task for the intellectual world in general. One of Dennett's major roles is in removing philosophical hindrances so that intellectuals of all stripes can get on with their work of building one integrated understanding of our world, natural and human.

Dennett's philosophy should be seen as a whole. His ultimate goal is to synthesize, after three centuries of standoff, the scientific and humanistic worldviews. Each of the following chapters, then, should be thought of as a piece of the jigsaw puzzle: what we are after is the integrated picture that reveals how all aspects of the biological and human worlds can be integrated coherently into one naturalistic worldview.

OUTLINE

Dennett's project of naturalism starts in the philosophy of mind. The basic problem with explaining consciousness is that we are captive to a mistaken story: the myth of the Cartesian Theater. To be conscious, according to this story, is for the conscious subject to have some real mental entity present before it, a representation or image of an object in the world or, in the empiricist version, a sense datum, a "quale." His most influential work, *Consciousness Explained*, is a sustained attack on this myth. Chapter 2 introduces his hetero-phenomenological method, and presents the arguments he offers to undermine the myth.

Chapter 3 will outline Dennett's alternative account of con-sciousness: the Multiple Drafts Model. Consciousness is a con-struct based on language and context. The question of whether this account implies that consciousness is real or illusionary will then have to be addressed.

For a naturalist, mind and consciousness must have evolved to serve some biological purpose, even if, in the end, they can transcend their biological origin. Like any biological function, we can only understand consciousness when we grasp how it has come into being. Dennett, who considers Darwin's theory of evolution to be one of the most important intellectual advances, uses adaptationism—the survival of the fittest—to explain mind, self, freedom, ethics, and religion. Indeed, Dennett holds that adaptation can be understood as a mode of explanation, a formal algorithm that is neutral with respect to the medium. Adaptation therefore occurs not only in bio-logical contexts, but in informational contexts (computer viruses, artificial life), and—critically important in the case of the mind—in cultural contexts. These issues will be examined in Chapter 4.

Chapter 5 applies Dennett's theory of consciousness, and his adaptationist method to the understanding of selfhood. Evolution-ary processes, both biological and cultural, form the foundation for the self. All organisms have some kind of unity, but the evolution of language opened the way for humans to represent their bodies, behaviors, and mental states to themselves. Typically this self-representation takes the form of a narrative, a story couched in language, in which the self is the leading protagonist. A human self is therefore a creature of culture and, especially, of language.

Is the self, then, a fiction? It all depends on what we mean by "real." In Chapter 6 we will face this central question, postponed in Dennett's accounts of consciousness, evolutionary constructs, and selfhood. Some philosophers want to reduce these phenom-ena to the concrete reality of physical processes. Others think of them as emergent realities. Dennett holds that there are differ-ent kinds or levels of reality, each dependent in a certain way on one of three epistemic strategies, or "stances," as he calls them: the physical; the design; and the intentional stance. Opposing what he calls "industrial strength realism"—the idea that there is only one kind of reality—Dennett defends what he labels "mild realism." Ultimately, the world is made up of multiple patterns of information and the role of each stance is to reveal different entities and properties of the world picked out by each strategy. The reality of objects is not then a feature solely of the objects themselves, but is dependent upon the perspective or method that we approach the world with.

In Chapter 7 we return from the abstractions of ontology to the more concrete issue of free will. Within the worldview of natural science, it is usually assumed that, since all events are causally determined by implacable laws, there is no place for human freedom. We should not be surprised by now to find Dennett arguing that, far from being opposed to each other, freedom and physical determinism are not only compatible, but the latter is a necessary condition for the former. We have in the past been mystified by an absolutist, metaphysical notion of freedom, but if the kind of freedom that we really want is understood as self-control, then we can find room for it within naturalism. Further, this notion allows Dennett to offer an account of the evolution of freedom as a biological and cultural adaptation.

Evolutionary thinking also allows Dennett to give an account of the emergence of ethical values from a purely biological world. As usual, he insists that ethical values really are valuable, as opposed to those who would dismiss them as illusions, but he also resists any attempt to withdraw them from their historical and evolutionary context and place them on some eternal, absolute pedestal. His antiabsolutism can also be found in his insistence that religion is a natural phenomenon and so should be studied objectively by science. He speculates on the kind of account that might emerge from this investigation: in the early days, various cultural features coalesce into a cluster that evolves into institutional religion as we know it today. Whether the result is good or bad for us is a question that must be examined head-on as we face the future. These value issues form the content of Chapter 8.

The final chapter summarizes the central themes of Dennett's philosophy and points briefly to potential areas of criticism.

CHAPTER 2

WHAT CONSCIOUSNESS IS NOT: THE CRITIQUE OF CARTESIANISM

Dennett is most famous for his account of consciousness. Given the general approach of his philosophy outlined above in the introduction, we can already anticipate the main lines of his argument. He acknowledges as valid the experience we all have of being conscious. He attacks, however, the theoretical understanding of it offered by dualists like Descartes. Nevertheless, he is just as unwilling to accept the position, maintained by some materialists, that consciousness is a pure illusion, a myth of popular culture and folk psychology. The two dichotomous positions are closer than they may appear: they share a common understanding of the nature of mental reality, though one affirms its existence while the other denies it. Dennett wants to offer us an alternative way to think about mental reality in the first place, one that allows us to avoid the traditional dichotomy.

The myth of the Cartesian Theater encapsulates and symbolizes this traditional picture of the mental that holds many of us captive: to be conscious is for some inner self, an ego, to have present before it in some kind of internal space a mental entity that somehow represents objects and events in the real world. The myth is endemic and shows up in many different guises even among people who think themselves immune to it; Dennett therefore painstakingly analyzes how the myth distorts our thinking, often in surprising ways. The next chapter will present Dennett's positive account of consciousness; but first we must look at his many-pronged attack on the Cartesian Theater.

In this chapter, I will first explain the myth to be attacked by laying out relevant features of Cartesian dualism and of its materialist twin, Cartesian materialism. After explaining Dennett's heterophe-nomenological method, we will be in a position to present his main reasons for rejecting the myth, in particular, his arguments against representationalism, or "real seeming," as he calls it.

CARTESIAN DUALISM

Descartes, in the early 17th century, was concerned to establish a solid foundation for the new mechanistic sciences in the face of the prevailing Aristotelianism and of fundamentalist opposition from the Inquisition. He therefore focused on the notion of certainty. At least two enemies of certainty concerned him: biases from tra-ditional beliefs that bear on us from culture, learning, authority and, very importantly, language; and deception due to the inade-quacies of our bodily systems of perception. He believed he could achieve certainty within a novel realm he calls *mens*, or mind. The certainty that a self-reflective subject has of his or her own exis-tence, the *cogito*, is the first step. The freedom of the subject to rec-ognize truth—a freedom that he equates with God's—comes from Descartes' realization that no cause, whether divine or mechanis-tic, could make him be in error about those clear and distinct ideas that he grasps within his mind by the natural light, e.g., that he is a thinking being. This separation of the mind from the causal order, be it divine or material, is the essence of Descartes' dualism.

Dualism permits Descartes to offer a solution to the problem of perceptual error. A tower looks differently to me and to you. Which of us is right? What is the truth about how the tower itself truly is, apart from its differing appearances in various perspectives? From a distance the tower looks small, though in reality it is large. There is even a possibility that the tower is a hallucination. I cannot how-ever be mistaken about my *idea* of the tower for, whether the exter-nal tower exists or not, I have a privileged, private, and indubitable grasp of the idea because it is interior to my mind. The mind is only in contact with itself, with its own contents. It is the immediate presence of content to the mind—intuition—that is the guarantee of certainty. This solution to the problem of perceptual uncertainty, however, brings with it a new difficulty: how can I be sure that the internal mental representation of the tower corresponds accurately to the real tower in the external world? Ultimately Descartes can solve this problem only by appealing to faith in God.

The internal certainty of intuition also solves the problem of bias from language and culture. Within the mental realm I see, that is, I have direct access to, the ideas themselves rather than receiving these ideas second-hand, mediated through the words of others. I may later use words to describe my experience, but the ideas that I am conscious of, that are present before me, are prior to language and so immune from any linguistic influence. First I see and then I speak.

Descartes' certainty also requires that each intuition be isolated or atomic. In so far as I intuit each individual idea present to me, I grasp its intrinsic nature regardless of my other experiences or beliefs. What I have before me is a triangle or a chiliagon (a thousand-sided figure); no context is needed for my immediate recognition of this essence. My immediate recognition of what it is I am experiencing does not depend on any wider context, either synchronous or temporal. What the subject is, what the object is, and the relationship between them is independent of anything beyond themselves.

The terms that Descartes uses for this relationship—intuiting, seeing, perceiving, and so on—suggest that Descartes is modelling the relationship between the ego and its ideas on the external relationship of the body to its visually perceived objects. It is as if the mental subject were a miniature person, a "homunculus," looking at an internal stage or screen on which the representations are displayed. It is this model that Dennett labels the "Cartesian Theater." A significant part of Dennett's work in the philosophy of mind, already in *Content and Consciousness*, but especially in *Consciousness Explained*, is a sustained criticism of every aspect of this picture. He criticizes the homunculus, the notion of representations as images, the screen on which they are displayed, the non-contextual and atomic nature of the experiences, the independence from language and culture, and the very notion of an appearing mental object itself—a "real seeming."

Before moving to these criticisms, which make up the bulk of this chapter, let me comment that Cartesian dualism as so described is of course a caricature. Internal, duplicating images of the real world are the kind of Aristotelian forms that Descartes himself was trying to overthrow. Descartes maintains that the mind is not spatial, so he cannot have intended to suggest that there is a homunculus viewing a screen from a distance; indeed even the spatial terms "internal" and "external" are, he occasionally points out, analogies (though he never does tell us what they are analogies for). Above all, Descartes was concerned to differentiate between images that have the same form as objects in the world and so are spatially articulated and ultimately bodily, from ideas that are abstract, conceptual, and quantifiable and therefore suitable as the foundations for science. He also toyed, rather unsuccessfully, with interactionism and he speculated quite extensively on the union of the body and soul—both elements that modify drastically, perhaps even undermine, "Cartesian" dualism.

"Cartesian" dualism is therefore a caricature of Descartes' own position. The caricaturing, however, cannot be laid at Dennett's feet. It is the received position accepted by those that Dennett inveighs against. It is the "Cartesian" idea of the mind that dualists defend and eliminativists reject. Even those who denounce Cartesian mind-body dualism in principle often unsuspectingly remain captive to many of the essential features of Descartes' scheme. They still cling to the idea that consciousness can be understood as one special place where "it all comes together"—where some homunculus still gazes at representations passing in the theater—though they assume that this place is to be found in the material brain. Dennett calls these thinkers "Cartesian materialists." His arguments are directed as much against them as against traditional dualists.

The traditional dualist picture has been gradually eroded since the 17th century by the progress of science, especially of the sciences that apply scientific method to human phenomena. The development of psychiatry, neurophysiology, and other brain sciences in the 19th and 20th centuries demonstrated unequivocally that mental phenomena were subject to causal laws and so are part of the realm of nature. This development strengthened the line of thought—eliminative materialism—that runs through Thomas Hobbes and Baron d'Holbach, to our contemporaries Patricia and Paul Churchland. According to this approach, causal mechanism governs everything in the world, so the very idea that there is a mental realm that escapes such laws must be rejected. The idea of a mental process is a figment of folklore, an attempt by prescientific thought to account for behaviors that ultimately must be described and explained in physiological terms. There can be no scientific, objective method of investigating consciousness or other mental phenomena since, in the end, they do not exist.

For Dennett, eliminative materialism and Cartesian dualism are two sides of the same coin. Both share a common understanding of mental reality and it is this concept that is his ultimate target. Before we can get at it, however, we must deal with a preliminary obstacle, a methodological scruple: both dualists and eliminativists agree that there is no objective method for studying consciousness. Dennett disagrees. He has such a method: heterophenomenology.

HETEROPHENOMENOLOGY

At first sight, it does indeed seem that conscious experience, the very epitome of the subjective, could never be studied objectively. Maybe individuals can use introspection to observe their own first-person experience, but how could they know whether their findings apply to other people? Is communication to others about what is essentially private not in principle impossible? Attempts in the late 19th century to establish a scientific psychology based on introspection are reputed to have found the method unreliable, and Dennett agrees. He labels this first-person method "autophenomenology," considers it unpromising as a scientific method, and proposes instead that we adopt his "heterophenomenology." (Dennett occasionally attributes the method of autophenomenology to Husserl, the founder of phenomenology. Husserl, aware of the introspective method, explicitly repudiates it, and goes to pains to distinguish his own "phenomenology" from it.)

The aim of Dennett's heterophenomenological method is to provide replicable, third-person, empirical data about consciousness, data based on objective observation. Dennett notes that many psychological and neurophysiological investigations on humans rely upon language. The investigator gives a subject instructions in a language she believes the subject understands, and gathers reports couched in language from subject. "Tell me when you see Waldo!" "I see Waldo now." (Or the subject may press a button that, it has been agreed in advance, means the same thing.) Heterophenomenology systematizes this process by recording the sounds made by a speaker describing how her experience seems to her. These sound recordings are then given to a number of native speakers of the language (say it is English) who interpret the sounds as meaningful sentences in English and then type them up in a written report. The stenographers may not agree. If one stenographer types, "I saw a dead pot," and another types, "I saw a red dot," then we jettison the reports. When the typescripts *can* be reliably replicated—when everyone agrees that what the speaker said is, "I saw a green light"—then we have a set of objective data to work with. We now have a scientific basis for asserting that the speaker seems to see a green light, or, as Dennett puts it, a green light is an object in the speaker's heterophenomenological world.

Dennett uses a well-known psychological experiment as an example: the "phi phenomenon." In a dark room a subject is presented with a brief spot of light followed rapidly by a second spot slightly further to the right. If the timing is right, the subject says she sees one spot moving from the left to the right. (This illusion is the basis for movies.) If our heterophenomenological stenographers all agree that the sounds made by the subject should be interpreted as reporting a single spot that moves, then we have an objective report of how it seems to her, of the presence of a moving spot in her heterophenomenological world.

This example brings out a crucial feature of the method: the privilege of the speaker. The speaker gets the final word: she is the absolute authority about the objects and events in her heterophenomenological world, about how things seem to her. The investigator may know what is real in the laboratory—that there are really two separate spots some milliseconds apart—but this knowledge must be suspended, for it has no role to play in the heterophenomenological report. With respect to how things seem to the speaker, that is, to consciousness, objects and events in the real world are irrelevant and must not be allowed to intrude. Dennett uses two analogies in explaining this methodological suspension. First, in fictional worlds created by authors, such as Conan Doyle, what the author says goes. So there are trains in Sherlock Holmes' London, since Doyle refers to them, but there are no aircraft because they are never mentioned. The second analogy is with cultural worlds studied by anthropologists. Consider the (hypothetical) world of a jungle people who believe in the god Feenoman. An anthropologist must take the informants' word with respect to who Feenoman is, and what role he plays in the affairs of the culture. Whether he is mischievous or a model of propriety is a question over which the participants in the culture have absolute authority. No outsider can overrule their judgement about what is true or false in their world. The point of these two analogies is to grant to the heterophenomenological reporter the same absolute right to say how things are in the hetero-phenomenological world as authors and informants have about how things are in fictional or cultural worlds. To say that such reporters must be given the last word is to say that no one else, not even a scientific observer of brain states, could ever overrule them.

The reporter's privilege is, however, limited to how things seem to her. She has no privilege with respect to explaining why things seem that way, about what is really happening in her brain, or about theoretical explanations for any of these events. One of the main functions of the heterophenomenological method is to drive a wedge between how things seem to the reporter and any theory the reporter might have about how they come to seem that way, that is, their causes. If she is a Cartesian, for example, she may theorize that the reason it seems to her that the spots change color is because there is a homunculus somewhere within her observing representational spots changing color in a Cartesian Theater. She has no privileged authority about the truth of that theory, nor about any other.

The heterophenomenological method delivers objective data about how things seem to the reporter, but remains strictly neutral with respect to what is really going on inside her. Indeed it remains neutral with respect to the question of whether anything mental is really going on at all or not. In principle, if there were a sophisticated computer that, without relying on consciousness, was able to generate sounds that our English-speaking stenographers could interpret coherently and consistently as referring to objects in a heterophenomenological world, the computer and its text would have the same privilege, as well as the same limitations. This is exactly what the investigation requires, for Dennett's philosophical problems include not only the nature of consciousness, but whether or not consciousness exists in the first place. A method with a set of objective observational data that is neutral on these questions is exactly what is needed.

One implication of the heterophenomenological method must not be missed: the data it delivers are semantic, i.e., meaningful, data. The typed reports do not concern themselves with the physical properties of the sounds the speaker makes: their frequencies, volume, harmonic structure, etc. What they offer us are assertions expressed in language. Our stenographers do not simply reproduce sounds; they interpret them as language about objects and events.

We are no longer dealing with purely physical entities but with the content referred to by linguistic symbols. The stenographers take a linguistic stance: their reports are interpretations of the meaning or significance of the sounds emitted by the original speaker, sounds that they take as utterances. We have already seen, of course, that almost all psychological experiments with humans presuppose that they are using language meaningfully, but this is a particularly important point when we are investigating consciousness. When Dennett refers to "how things seem to the speaker," he is referring to the interpreted content of linguistic utterances. The heterophenomenological method ties consciousness very tightly to language.

This simple step is freighted with implications; we move by it from one world—the world of mere sounds—into another: the world of words and meanings, syntax and semantics. This step yields a radical reconstrual of the data, an abstraction from its acoustic and other physical properties to strings of words. . . . (CE 74–75)

Dennett's heterophenomenology differs from Descartes' approach in that he substitutes for the Cartesian structure of an intuiting subject facing intuited objects the alternative structure of a speaker and things spoken about. The heterophenomenological world is the set of objects and events that the speaker speaks of. Dennett claims that this moves the discussion of experience from a first-person point of view to an objective, third-person account. Yet it is just as important to note that it moves from a perceptual model built on analogy with visual perception to a semantic model based on analogy with language. The speaker and the spoken-of replace the seer and the seen. The result may be third-person objective, but it is not a physical objectivity: it is not the measurement of sound-wave parameters that is involved, but semantic objectivity about what the speaker means. Dennett argues that many uncontestedly objective psychological investigations depend on the meaning of language. "When you see it, push this button," plays an essential part in many experiments, but the part it plays depends on its meaning, not on the sound waves involved. Offering the semantically identical instructions in writing, which from the point of view of physics would be entirely different, leaves the experiment unchanged. If the involvement of semantics in common psychological experiments is uncontested, then the objectivity of heterophenomenology should be equally acceptable.

The significance of Dennett's heterophenomenological method is twofold. First, against those who suggest that he dismisses consciousness as an illusion, it allows him to acknowledge the richness of conscious experience, of how things seem to us. Secondly, against those who consider his approach unscientific, he can point to the replicable data of the heterophenomenological report. That the report is semantic makes it no less objective or third-person than many other psychological experiments that gave linguistic instructions to the subject.

THE CARTESIAN THEATER

Dennett now has a method, heterophenomenology, for investigating consciousness. He uses this method to attack the Cartesian myth about mental realities. Since the myth is so embedded in the way we think about the mind, even when we think about it in a scientific context, Dennett needs to expose its pernicious influence in many different contexts and so gradually disarm its power over us. He therefore attacks the myth from a number of different directions. In the rest of this chapter, I will discuss half a dozen of these arguments, beginning with the simplest and moving to the more radical.

Let me start by considering the notion of a perspective. An iceberg may be tracked from above by a satellite. I may get a different point of view on the same iceberg by sailing around it in a ship. Even on the ship I can change perspectives: I can stop looking from the cold deck, go up to the warm bridge and watch it through the windscreen. The iceberg is out there in the sea; my point of view is from inside the bridge. It would be a fundamental mistake, thinks Dennett, if this notion of perspective were to be taken "all the way in." At a stretch, we might say that my brain has a point of view on the iceberg from behind my eyes, but we certainly can't say my optical lobes have a perspective on the iceberg.

Attributions like these work only globally. A thief cannot excuse himself by claiming, "it was my hand that did it": blame can only apply to the whole person. The case of visual perspective is similar. Although various circuits in the brain may be involved in my perspectival view of the iceberg, they cannot be said themselves to have a perspective. Only I as a whole person have a perspective. The Cartesian myth mistakenly thinks that the notion of perspective can be "taken all the way in" and used to describe what goes on in some internal headquarters, the theater of the mind: a homunculus with a certain perspective on an iceberg-image on the screen. Such a homunculus itself would have to be spatial and have a point of view. Should we then hypothesize a point of view from within the homunculus? Does it too have a further inner screen with a smaller homunculus watching it? If we are to avoid an infinite regress, at some stage we just have to stop with a global attribution that cannot be taken any further in. Dennett's claim is that the point at which we should stop is the person as a whole. Mental and brain structures may be involved in the having of visual perspectives, but that no more means that these structures themselves have a point of view than that the involvement of the mouth in making promises means that the mouth promises.

The error is to take models and concepts that make sense in understanding the everyday world and to push them inward and apply them to our understanding of consciousness where they no longer make sense. We will meet this error time and again in Dennett's critique; he does not give it a name, so let me call it the "taking-it-all-the-way-in" error.

Descartes' own fundamental error is very similar. In our everyday understanding of visual perception, there are two poles: here is the body with its visual capacities on the one side, doing the seeing; there on the other side, are things seen, i.e., objects that are real in their own right independently of being seen. Our vision just chances upon them. The Cartesian Theater is the application of this external model to the understanding of consciousness. The viewer is replaced by the ego or homunculus, while the objects seen are replaced by mental images or representations present before it. It is this internalization of the model of visual perception that provokes the analogy of the Cartesian Theater: a one-person audience gazing at images on a screen. (Dennett is using "theater" in the American sense of a movie theater, a cinema.) The analogy naturally leads us to think of the images on the screen remaining the way they are even if the viewer falls asleep, looks away, or fails to pay attention. It also suggests that the viewer could be mistaken about what is really on the screen. (Descartes himself, of course, rejected these implications; this is a caricature, remember!)

Materialists who reject the notions of ego and mental representation are not thereby immune to this fundamental error. Consider how a neurophysiologist might talk about vision. Peripheral nerves on the retina input information from the eye to the optical lobes of the brain where it is processed by unconscious neural mechanisms that process the shape, color, position, distance, movement, facial characteristics, and so on. These various streams of processing must then be brought together in one place, perhaps with additional input from object and social categorizers, memory, and other processes—Central Headquarters, as it were—where the inputs can all be integrated and where decisions can be made, decisions that govern the neural impulses that flow back down to the periphery to control the muscles. This is the Continental Divide; it is upstream of all afferent sensations; and it is the point where all downstream, efferent impulses originate. When discussing the nervous system, Descartes himself suggested that the pineal gland was such a center. Just as the captain on the bridge of a ship integrates optical, sonar and radar inputs and sends out executive commands to the rudder and engines, so we conceive of a "bridge" in the brain where the input is centrally assessed and decisions are made. This notion that consciousness occurs at a single place where "everything comes together" is the materialist equivalent of the Cartesian Theater. Dennett thinks this materialist version is just as mistaken as the dualist one.

This is one version of the myth. "The place where it all comes together" is conceived of as a brain location, a functional cognitive space, or a mental point. It is this mythical place that Dennett labels a theater. Both dualists and hardnosed materialistic neurophysiologists are both stuck with this picture of consciousness. Recognizing it is the first step to disarming its power over us.

A related way that Dennett tries to break the stranglehold of the Cartesian picture is by discussing the vision system of Shakey the robot. A video camera allows Shakey to distinguish objects in a room so that they can be manipulated. Shakey's software program allows it to process the video image by identifying the edges of objects, analyzing the vertices of these line drawings and then categorizing them as boxes, pyramids, and so on. The programmers conveniently arrange that the steps in this process are projected onto a screen so that the investigators can monitor what is happening. The observers can then see a sequence of images progressing from a grainy videocam picture, to a simplified line drawing of light-dark boundaries, and then to a clearly identified box.

Shakey, of course, does not look at the monitor; its cameras are focused on the objects in the room. The images that appear on the screen are for the benefit of the observers. If we disconnect the monitor so that there are no images anywhere in the system, Shakey identifies and manipulates objects exactly as before. Inside Shakey the input from the video cameras is initially recorded as a series of pixels whose value is either zero or one and whose addresses are also series of binary numbers. These digits are recorded magnetically on a hard drive. In the early stages of processing, the linear string of zeros and ones has no color or orientation, but it may still have a pattern that has some isomorphic relationship to the spatial structure of the box. Should we call it an "image?" Perhaps in an analogous use of the term we can, but it is not a real visual image. After the image has been categorized as a box, it should be particularly evident that the sequence of zeros and ones encoding this information has no resemblance whatsoever to the spatial structure of the box itself.

The analogy with Optical Character Recognition software may be enlightening for those familiar with such programs. A page of text is scanned on a flatbed scanner and the program records the color value, e.g., black or white, of each pixel scanned. This is the bitmap, perhaps in the format of a jpg or bmp file. This stream of binary digits is then fed into the OCR program that recognizes patterns of pixels as printed letters and translates them into ASCII code. The binary bits in the ASCII code have no relationship whatever to the spatial arrangement of the pixels in the bitmap that make up the original letters. In an analogous way the visual system (robotic or human) encoding a box employs elements that do not form a spatial replica of the physical box. The bitmap stage might be referred to as an image, with some stretching of the term; but the term image cannot be applied literally to either the ASCII code or the encoding for the box.

In order to troubleshoot Shakey's system, the designers could add second-order diagnostic programs to monitor how well the processing is going. This may enable observers to ask Shakey questions like, "Do you have the line-drawing image yet?" If Shakey answers, "Yes, I have that image," how should we interpret this? In one sense it must be false, since, given the design of the system,

Shakey has no images inside it. Still, it might be natural for the troubleshooters to take Shakey at his word and say, "Shakey believes he can see the line-drawing image," and for them to assume that Shakey's belief is true. (If it is not, there is some error in the diagnostic program.)

The second-order monitoring could reach down to various levels of detail, depending on the interests of the troubleshooters. So if they inquire of Shakey how it identifies a box, it could reply in a number of different ways. It might say it takes the zeros and ones from the video bit-mapping and processes them through programs X, Y, Z, etc. to identify certain patterns that other programs A, B, C, etc. process in order to identify the box—a long story. If the diagnostic program produced less detail, Shakey might just report, "I find the light-dark boundaries and draw white lines around them in my mind's eye; then I look for the shape of vertices that allow me to identify a box." If the diagnostic program is particularly skimpy, Shakey may just reply, "I aim my video camera at the object and somehow I just know immediately that it is a box." He might add, "It just seems that way to me." It is up to the designers to decide how much access Shakey's reporting capacity should have to his perceptual processes.

From a heterophenomenological point of view we can now distinguish between how things seem to Shakey as we interpret its reports and how they really are in Shakey's processing. If Shakey says that it just seems like a box to him, we can grant that is true even though we know that in fact there is more to the story than what he is able to report. Similarly if Shakey's report is that he manipulates images in his mind's eye, we can grant him the truth of that statement even while we know, on a more technical level, that the "images" that he is referring to are really a sequence of zeros and ones.

There are three points we can take away from this scenario. First, the brain may represent objects in the world by encoding, which means that there is not necessarily any structure within the brain that has the same spatial properties as the object. One component of the Cartesian myth is that on the inner screen there must be a representation that is a replica of the external object. The Shakey scenario may loosen the power of this conviction. The brain can represent an object without replicating its shape.

Secondly, the scenario explains how a heterophenomenological reporter may not have access to the mechanisms by which something appears the way it does. She may be able to say that something seems like a box to her without being able to explain how this comes about. When it comes to self-description of our cognitive processes, our capacities may be quite limited.

Finally, it follows that the objects that a reporter refers to in a heterophenomenological world may actually, in the reality of the brain, have a different nature than the report indicates. In principle, the report could be a pure confabulation. "I use my TV input to drive an internal chisel that hews a box out of mental clay." As Dennett puts it:

> There are circumstances in which people are just wrong about what they are doing and how they are doing it. It is not that they *lie* in the experimental situation, but that they confabulate; they fill in the gaps, guess, speculate, mistake theorizing for observing. (CE 94)

> To sum up, subjects are unwitting creators of fiction, but to say that they are unwitting is to grant that what they say is, or can be, an account of *exactly how it seems to them*. They tell us *what it is like* to them to solve the problem, make the decision, recognize the object. Because they are sincere (apparently), we grant that that must be what it is like to them, but then it follows that what it is like to them is at best an uncertain guide to what is going on in them. (CE 94)

While the heterophenomenological report itself cannot be challenged, its indubitability covers only how things seem to the reporter. Any speculation the reporter offers about how things come to seem that way is not privileged. In the case of the phi phenomenon, for instance, when a reporter claims that the reason it seems to her that there is a single dot moving is because she has observed an inner image of a moving dot, we can simply discount this claim as part of the theoretical commitment that comes with her belief in the Cartesian Theater. Some people try to defend the myth by saying that they actually experience internal, mental representations. The Shakey scenario allows Dennett to reject this line of argument. That it seems to the reporter that the dot is moving cannot be challenged; the theory that the seeming is caused by a moving mental dot is an unfounded theoretical speculation.

Another argument that Dennett uses to loosen the grip of the Cartesian Theater is to examine our experience of color.

My eye lights upon a red tomato on a green tomato plant. My retina sends the information to my optical lobes where the shape analyzers distinguish the circular tomato against the background of the plant while, in a parallel process, my color discriminators recognize the redness of one area in contrast with the greenness of the other. What happens next? According to the Cartesian myth, my brain must send both streams of information to the Cartesian Theater where the tomato shape must be projected on the screen and the red color filled in, so that the two streams of information can be integrated by the homuncular ego becoming conscious of the red tomato. But this story must be nonsense. With what does the brain fill in the color? Surely not with oil pigments! Dennett proposes that we should call the mental filling-in "figment" to emphasize how ludicrous this story is. With the possible exception of some red blood cells, there is nothing red in the brain. Even if there were some red figment, the skull is opaque, so there would be no light to reflect off it.

Even if this mythical story were true, what function would the process serve? The color has already been recognized as red by the color discriminators, so this information is already available to the brain. Why would the homunculus have to gaze at the screen and recognize the redness all over again? And would it need a second set of color discriminators internal to the homunculus to do this? What we need is not filling-in, but finding-out, and this has already been accomplished.

A much more likely theory is that, once the discrimination is made the first time, the information is encoded—"it's red"—and made available to any other processes that need it. Perhaps my hunger has primed my motor cortex to pick and eat anything I can identify as a tomato, so the encoded information will be used to guide these actions. Perhaps the information will be used to activate the word "tomato" in my language module so that I can report that what I see is a tomato. If I am part of a heterophenomenological investigation, I may be led to say, "I seem to see a red tomato." In any of these cases, what is needed is the information, "It's red," the result of the earlier discrimination; what is not needed is a red representation whose color would have to be analyzed all over again.

In this case, as often, the Cartesian myth makes the mistake of failing to attribute the perception of the red tomato to the perceiver as a whole. It is I, this total individual, who perceives and is conscious of the red tomato, and who can express this experience in a verbal report and in other ways. I accomplish this by means of various internal processes, but it makes no sense to attribute perception to any of these component parts. The hypothesizing of imaginary figment filling in a shape on the screen is a consequence of attributing perception to an inner homunculus rather than to the global self.

Once again, a computer analogy is useful. In processing colored images, computers encode the color of each pixel and use these encodings to analyze the images, to reproduce them on a monitor or to transmit them to other computers. The computer, however, does not encode this information by painting parts of the hard drive red!

So we can conclude that the hypothesis of a mental representation that is really colored is as unreasonable as the claim that Shakey had a real, geometrically shaped image of a box.

THE ABSENCE OF REAL PRESENCE

Behind Dennett's rejection of the filling in of color by figment, of the existence of spatial images in Shakey, and of the idea of taking the notion of perspective all the way in is a more fundamental issue. It is not just that these errors assign the wrong content to mental realities. What Dennett rejects is a theory of consciousness that proposes *any* inner representations actually present before the mind. Examining a number of other perceptual experiences will enable us to see some of the reasons against this myth of real presence.

Consider the game of "hide the thimble." A thimble is "hidden" in plain view somewhere in a cluttered room. The player must spot it. Those standing around can often see that the player is looking directly at the thimble but failing to recognize it. Indeed once the thimble has popped out at him, the player can remember looking directly at the scene with the thimble without spotting it. What would a proponent of the Cartesian Theater have to say? Before the thimble has been found, is the thimble-representation present on or absent from the Cartesian screen? Could the homunculus fail to see something on the inner screen before him? The myth insists that for something to be conscious is just for it to be on the screen, but the player reports having been conscious of the same scene beforehand while still being unaware of the thimble. The claim that consciousness can be analyzed as presence on the screen is inadequate.

Look at another case. The visual field is colored, at least for those of us who are not color-blind. It seems as if it is colored from one periphery to the other. Yet if you stare straight ahead while someone moves a colored playing card from directly behind you into your peripheral field, you are unable to say what color it is. Try it! The card can be moved surprisingly close to the center of your visual field before you can name the color. Since most of us know already that only the cones of the macula are sensitive to color while the rods on the rest of the retina are not, we should not be surprised by this experience. Yet we are surprised! It seems to us that the whole visual field is colored, though only the center of it really is. By the visual field, of course, we do not mean the real physical world that is colored even behind our backs; we mean the visual world in so far as we are conscious of it. But what does that mean? If we try to explain it by saying that the visual field is what appears on our Cartesian screen then we have a problem: Is the periphery of the scene on the screen colored or not? If it is really colored, then we must be conscious of the color of the card that appears peripherally, since, according to the Cartesian view, being on the screen is what it means to be conscious. Yet, in fact, we are not aware of the color. The Cartesian has to say that the card-representation on the theater screen seems to be colored but really is not. Yet the claim is that the whole screen is how things seem to us. Do we now have to distinguish between what seems to seem colored and what really seems colored? The reason for invoking the Cartesian screen in the first place is to explain the difference between how things really are in the world and how they seem to us; far from explaining this distinction, we have now simply re-duplicated the problem internally.

The same conclusion can be reached by looking at "change blindness." A subject contemplates a scene on a computer screen, with plenty of time to examine all its parts. The screen flickers and a similar image appears with some significant change; for example, on a street there may be only three lampposts where there were four before. The subject reports seeing no change. The two scenes may be flipped many times before what is happening dawns on the subject. The recognition of the change cannot be accounted for simply by the presence or absence of the lamppost in the Cartesian Theater. (Try it yourself: http://en.wikipedia.org/wiki/Change_blindness.)

Here is yet another example for which the "presence on an inner screen" analysis fails. If you look at a wallpaper with a repetitive pattern—for instance, repeated images of Marilyn Monroe—are you conscious of all the repeated images? If being conscious means presence on your inner screen, then since you certainly seem to be conscious of all the images, they must all be present on the screen. Experimental evidence shows, however, that if during a "saccade"—one of the rapid involuntary movements of the eye from one part of the scene to another that occur constantly—one of the repeated images is changed, perhaps Nelson Mandela is substituted for Marilyn Monroe, you will probably be totally unaware of the change. The changed image is sitting there before you, sticking out like a sore thumb, as one might say, yet you remain unconscious of it.

What does this mean for consciousness? Dennett suggests that no image of the wallpaper (or of any visual scene) is present in some theater of consciousness. Instead, you have available to you the results of many discriminations—unconscious judgements, as it were— that you can call upon when needed. While some of these discriminations are of the form, "There is a Marilyn Monroe on this patch of the wallpaper I just focused on," many are of the form, "and so on. . . ." This information is available to you to call on if you need to act or report, but it is not currently "present" to you like an image might be. Of course, it seems to you that you are conscious continually, but this seeming is a kind of artefact of commonsense theorizing. The change of one section of the wallpaper from Marilyn Monroe to Nelson Mandela may not have been updated in your coded information, so if you are called upon (even by yourself) to report on it you say, "It seems to me that the Marilyn Monroes are continuous," that is, you will say that you are conscious of a wallpaper made up entirely of Marilyn Monroes; that is what you are conscious of. Consciousness is not presence on a Cartesian screen, but current reportability.

Dennett's criticisms, so far, have been aimed at the notion of a single place where everything comes together. He is equally critical, however, of the idea that everything comes together at a single temporal moment. Descartes himself held that the certainty of the *cogito* was valid only for the present instant. A moment later, the experience of the *cogito* is a memory, and memories do not share in the absolute certainty of consciousness. Consciousness itself is instantaneous; it occurs at exactly one instant in time. Memory is a different matter; it is not consciousness.

To understand Dennett's criticism of this account, let us start with a variation on the phi phenomenon. Again the subject in the laboratory is presented with two, spatially separated, spots of light in rapid succession. This time, however, the spots are different colors, say, red and green. When we interpret the heterophenomenological report, we find that it seems to the subject not only, as before, that there is a single moving light, but that the light changes color halfway through its movement. This is surprising. How could the subject know, halfway through the movement, what color the ending spot is going to be? On the Cartesian screen, the second spot has not yet appeared, so the subject cannot be conscious of it. Yet somehow she must be in order for the spot to change color correctly.

Once again, the problem arises from thinking of consciousness as a single finish line in a cognitive race. As information is processed in the brain, some of it crosses the one and only finish line at which it becomes conscious; once over the line, it becomes memory. There is only one screen; information that appears on it has its moment of glory, it reaches consciousness, and is then immediately relegated to the archives. It is this picture of consciousness that Dennett wants to free us from.

Consider the following thought-experiment. On Monday someone tampers with your brain and inserts a bogus memory of a woman in a hat into your memory of a party you attended on Sunday. On Tuesday you may be conscious of a vivid memory of Sunday's party and swear that the experience includes the woman in the hat. Dennett describes such a rewriting of memory, of your history, as Orwellian, by analogy with the rewriting of history by the state in George Orwell's novel, *1984*. First, you actually have the experience, then, secondly, it is overwritten in your memory.

There is a different way you might be fooled. In the USSR, Stalin staged show trials with false testimony, invented evidence, corrupted confessions, and so on as part of a public disinformation campaign. These trials were real in the sense that they actually happened, though the events attested to in them were fabricated. History records the holding of the trials—accurately. In the everyday world there is a clear distinction between the Orwellian rewriting of history and the Stalinesque mode of misleading people.

THE CRITIQUE OF CARTESIANISM

In the Stalinesque case the corruption occurs before the experience of the trial; in the Orwellian case the corruption occurs after the experience.

Once again we can be misled if we take these distinctions, valid in the everyday world, import them into the brain and use them to analyze consciousness. This is the taking-it-all-the-way-in error. Imagine the following scenario. You have a friend who wears glasses. A different person, though similar, runs by who does not wear glasses. One second later your memory is contaminated by the image of your friend so that you mistakenly remember the runner as wearing glasses. You could swear that you saw glasses on her! This is an Orwellian event—it is the memory, not the experience, that is corrupted. However, things might go differently. Perhaps because you are actively thinking about your friend at this instant, your perception of the runner is contaminated by the addition of glasses before you experience her; you hallucinate the glasses. Once again, you could swear that you saw glasses on the runner!

In both cases your heterophenomenological report would be identical. You say, sincerely, that you were conscious of glasses on the runner. The Cartesian materialist must insist that, whatever you say, there is a fact of the matter: at the instant when the input all came together either there were glasses on the runner's face or there were not. Of course you cannot tell which. Unfortunately, given your privileged and exclusive access to that of which you are conscious, no one else can tell either. The Cartesian insists on the crucial distinction between the Orwellian and Stalinesque accounts. Dennett insists it is a distinction without a difference.

It is very important to understand that Dennett is not supporting the Orwellian account against the Stalinesque or vice versa. Both accounts are wrong and wrong for the same reason: both presuppose that what makes the experience conscious is that the data all come together at some privileged moment, the instant of consciousness. Both assume that there is a finish line that was crossed first by either a runner with glasses or a runner without glasses. The rest is memory. This is the Cartesian Theater, which Dennett is rejecting.

NO REAL SEEMING

For Dennett, the most fundamental mistake involved, in one way or another, in all of these cases of Cartesianism, is the belief in real seemings. All agree that how things are in the world is one thing; how they seem to us in consciousness is another. To account for the difference, the Cartesian proposes that consciousness is the presence to a subject of a mental entity that parallels and represents the real world, sometimes correctly sometimes incorrectly. Dennett grants that there may be a difference between how things really are and how they seem in consciousness; what he rejects is the idea of accounting for this difference by hypothesizing a second reality, a mental representation. In the phi phenomenon—to pursue this case—it seems to the subject that there is a single moving light when in reality there are two different fixed lights with a temporal delay. To explain the difference by inventing a mental moving light is to create a real seeming, and a time and place for it to exist, the Cartesian Theater. Nothing is really moving, insists Dennett; there is no such real seeming, no such mental representation.

The term "representation" can be confusing. Just as a thermometer tracks temperature changes, so there are brain processes that track how things are in the world. This tracking process may be called "representation." Dennett is not denying representations in this sense. The philosophical tradition, however, often uses the word "representation"—in German, "Vorstellung"—to refer to an object, a mental entity, that "stands before the mind," that "stands in" for—in the sense of standing in place of—a nonmental object that is being represented, much as a political representative might stand in for her constituents. This is the Cartesian sense that Dennett rejects. This is the "real seeming" that he thinks both Cartesian dualists and Cartesian materialists are fundamentally mistaken about.

A particularly insightful way of understanding Dennett's objection is to look at the representation of time. Dennett offers the following scenario: in 1814, in Belgium, British diplomats signed a truce ending the 1812 war with the United States. The information arrived too late to prevent hundreds being killed in the battle of New Orleans 15 days later. Other parts of the British Empire may have received news about the battle before hearing of the truce. Say there was a British official in India; he may have received a letter about the battle before getting a letter about the truce. Yet this official would not have been confused, for we have a custom of dating letters so that, although the letter about the truce might have arrived later than the one about the battle, it was date-stamped earlier.

In the order of information flow—the representing process—different parts of the Empire get the news at different times, yet in the order of information content—that which is represented—the truce date is the same everywhere.

In Dennett's analogy, information reaches different parts of the representing process in the brain at different times and there is no central Cartesian Theater or "instant" of consciousness. The time of consciousness is the time of the represented, of the date-stamp placed on the information. In the phi experiment, for instance, the point of time when the brain discriminates the change of color must occur after the second, green—the order of the representing process—but it gets date-stamped as occurring before it in the order of the represented. Hence in our heterophenomenological world, when we come to report it, it seems to us that the color change occurs before the green flash. The brain need not use the temporal order of the brain processes as the means of representing the temporal order of events in the world, hence the temporal relationships between brain processes that represent events need not be the same as the temporal relationships between the events represented. Cartesianism, dualist or materialist, identifies the temporality of consciousness with a moment in the brain, that is, in the representing process. A crucial mistake, claims Dennett: the temporal relationship between objects and events as we are conscious of them is a relationship within the represented.

The error occurs from confusing what is represented with the process or mechanism of representing it. In Shakey's case, the Cartesian mistakenly assumed that the representing must have the same spatial structure as the box represented; in fact, the representing is done by a string of binary digits that have no box-like spatial structure. In the case of color, it would be a mistake to assume that the redness of a rose is represented by some red-colored figment in the mind, on the Cartesian screen, or in the brain. In fact it is represented by encoded electrical signals in neural circuits whose color is irrelevant. In the wallpaper example, that there are a thousand Marilyns on the wall does not mean that there must be a thousand images on the screen. In change blindness, it is mistakenly taken for granted that change in the world must be represented by change on the screen, or in the brain or whatever. In the thimble case, it is assumed that the presence of the thimble in the world is represented by its presence on the screen. Dennett insists that "we distinguish representing from represented, vehicle from content" (CE 131). He assigns the representing to various brain processes and criticizes others for confusing the properties of these processes with the properties of the objects represented.

The mistake is not simply to assume that the properties of our mental representations are similar to properties of the real objects represented. It is more fundamental. We are not aware of any properties of mental representations; there are *no mental representations* that we are aware of. There are *no real seemings* whatsoever. There are no mental entities present to us. Consciousness represents the presence of objects in the world, but it does not do so by the presence of representations of these objects. As Dennett puts it:

> The absence of representation is not the same as the representation of absence. And the representation of presence is not the same as the presence of representation. But this is hard to believe. Our conviction that we are somehow *directly acquainted* with special properties or features in our experience is one of the most powerful intuitions confronting anyone trying to develop a good theory of consciousness. (CE 359)

Dennett's opposition to real seemings is not just the empirical claim that, as a matter of fact, there are no mental representations; it is a philosophical claim that the notion of mental representation is conceptually incoherent. In this regard, he describes himself as a "first-person operationalist." Some logical empiricists, in the first half of the 20th century, claimed that the meaning of scientific terms comes from the operations used to verify them. Temperature, for instance, could be defined as the number one got by observing a thermometer under specified conditions. A concept for which no operations of verification are specified is, they held, a meaningless concept, a nonscientific one. This is "third-person" operationalism and defines which concepts are meaningful for objective science. By mid-century, the position was generally rejected as untenable, and Dennett makes no attempt to defend the position in general. Yet he does think it makes admirable sense when applied to subjective experience.

In the case of subjective introspection, a reality is meaningful only if the subject can introspect it: defenders of real seemings insist that to describe them as "first-person" is precisely to say they cannot be detected by objective methods. Dennett's argument is that a real seeming is not only undetectable by objective methods; it cannot be verified on the basis of conscious experience either. In principle, all we can ever know about an individual's experience is what appears in their heterophenomenological report; indeed all that any individual can know about their own experience is how they judge it to be—what they report to themselves about it, as it were. So all that can be known within consciousness is how things are experienced, how they seem to us, and nothing else; if there were a mental reality-in-itself that brought about this seeming, we could never know it; we could never be conscious of it. But if a real seeming is, in principle, something that can be accessed neither objectively nor subjectively, then, says a first-person operationalist, the concept is strictly meaningless.

* * *

This chapter has been concerned with the primarily negative task of loosening the grip of a common philosophical picture of consciousness. Under the banner of "Cartesian Theater," Dennett has included a complex set of presuppositions: consciousness should be thought of along the model of perception; there are mental representations that represent states of the external world; such representations have properties similar to those of the objects represented; subjects have direct access to these mental entities; consciousness involves everything coming together at some privileged place and time. It is this cluster of ideas that make up the Cartesian account of consciousness, whether in its dualist or materialist version. Dennett uses the arguments above—and others I have not included—to soften up our commitment to this account and prepare us to accept an alternative notion. It is to this positive theory of consciousness that we must turn in the coming chapter.

CHAPTER 3

WHAT CONSCIOUSNESS IS:
THE MULTIPLE DRAFTS MODEL

Dennett's positive account of the nature of mind positions itself, as we already noted, on the middle ground between two extremes. On the one hand, he rejects approaches like eliminativism or identity theory that treat consciousness as illusory and reduce it to purely physical processes in the brain. On the other hand, he is equally opposed to those remnants of dualist thought, qualia and zombies—more on these below—that imply that consciousness is ultimately mysterious and cannot be integrated into the scientific worldview.

The middle position has been the preserve of "functionalism," and Dennett frequently aligns himself with this school of thought, so we will start by explaining the functionalist features of his philosophy. Yet, for Dennett, functionalism is but a step toward a more all-embracing contextualism, an approach we will look at by contrasting it with the notion of noncontextual qualia. We will then be ready to present Dennett's full-blown "Multiple Drafts Model" of consciousness and to show how it accounts for the "stream of consciousness." Finally, at the end of this chapter, we will discuss the crucial role of language: its generation; and its role in explaining consciousness.

FUNCTION

The idea of functionalism developed in the philosophy of mind in opposition to identity theory. Identity theory held that mental and neural processes were simply the same events under different names: just as "lightning" and "electrical discharge" named the same event—though the second may be scientifically more sophisticated—"pain" and "C-fiber firings" are identical. Functionalists (Putnam is often credited with initiating the approach around 1960) point out that aliens might well have radically different nervous systems than humans, but that that fact would hardly stand in the way of us attributing pain to such beings if, when we injured them, they complained that it hurt. Rather than being identical to any specific neural process, the mental experience we call pain could supervene on any number of different neural processes. What allows us to label a neural process as pain is not the nature of the physical event, but the role that this physical event plays in the larger economy of the organism as a whole, that is, its "function." Of course, in any particular instance, the function would have to be carried out by some concrete, physical, neural process. What makes it a pain, however, cannot be understood in terms of this material process, but only by reference to the more abstract role that this process plays in the overall cognitive structure. In principle, any particular kind of cognitive function—pain in our example—can be realized in any one of multiple possible ways. The multiple realizability of functions differentiates functionalism from identity theory while still allowing functionalists to account for mental events without invoking spirits, mental substances, or other nonmaterial entities.

Let me note, parenthetically, that I am speaking here, and throughout this book, about function in the narrow sense in which this term is used in the philosophy of mind. There is a broad sense of the term—the search for general, abstract regularities—in which every scientist is a functionalist. As Dennett puts it:

> [Broad] Functionalism is the idea that handsome is as handsome does, that matter matters only because of what matter can do. Functionalism in this broadest sense is so ubiquitous in science that it is tantamount to a reigning presumption of all of science. . . . The law of gravity says that it doesn't matter what stuff a thing is made of—only its mass matters. . . . (SD 17)

Dennett's functionalism (in the narrow sense of the term) differentiates him from behaviorists. Philosophical behaviorists—Gilbert Ryle, notably—restrict their analysis to overt and publicly observable behaviors. Mental attributes are treated as dispositions to behave. A behaviorist account of pain, to pursue this example, would go something like this: to say, "She has a pain in the hand that she put on a hot stove" can be translated into "She pulls her hand back, moves away from the source of the pain, says 'ouch!,' and refuses to go near the stove in future, etc." Dennett accepts the notion of disposition, but, unlike his mentor Ryle, is willing to also include psychological dispositions within the person. A cognitive "function" can be thought of as a kind of internal disposition: a mental experience is one of pain if it provokes a surge of anxiety, revives memories of previous painful events, interferes with the focus of one's philosophical thoughts, or other responses like these, whether or not it also leads to overt behaviors like withdrawing or crying out.

CONTEXT

Since function refers to the role an event plays in its context, function and context are always implicitly linked. Dennett, however, by interpreting cognitive functions along the lines of Rylean dispositions, makes context more explicit and establishes it as the defining feature of consciousness. A conscious state cannot be defined by an intrinsic essence: What makes a state conscious is the set of dispositions that it is linked to, that is to say, to the functional role it plays in the overall dynamics of the organism's life. Dennett's contextual and dispositional account of consciousness can be unpacked in four ways, which we will look at in turn: the rejection of qualia; the nature of pain; the phenomenon of blindsight; and the preposterousness of zombies.

The word "qualia" (singular "quale"), as Dennett understands it, designates

> the *ways things seem to us*. As is so often the case with philosophical jargon, it is easier to give examples than to give a definition of the term. Look at a glass of milk at sunset; *the way it looks to you*—the particular, personal, subjective visual quality of the glass of milk is the *quale* of your visual experience at the moment. The *way the milk tastes to you then* is another, gustatory *quale*, and *how it sounds to you* as you swallow is an auditory *quale*; These various "properties of conscious experience" are prime examples of *qualia*. Nothing, it seems, could you know more intimately than your own qualia; let the entire universe be

some vast illusion, some mere figment of Descartes' evil demon, and yet what the figment is *made of* (for you) will be the *qualia* of your hallucinatory experiences. (QQ)

While the notion is closely related to the Cartesian idea that when an ego is conscious there is something present to it, the simple, isolated nature of a quale comes not so much from Descartes as from the early Modern empiricist doctrine of sensationalism: all experience begins with sense data. Hume is a good illustration: he held that all ideas in the mind ultimately originate in simple impressions that are atomic in the sense that each one is independent of the others. The eye, for example, delivers to the mind simple sensations of red, green, or other colors that are then associated together by the mind to form our ideas of objects. Each individual sense datum has its own quality that identifies it and distinguishes it from other sense data. The distinctive, intrinsic quality of redness, for instance, is what determines that my experience of a red sense datum is red.

Functionalism is implausible to many because it seems to leave out this qualitative content of mental states. Over and above my external or internal dispositions to react to a mental state, I *experience* it. Are there not raw feels, impressions, or sensations; that is, does consciousness not involve intrinsic properties that I experience before I categorize them, make judgements about them, or respond in any way whatsoever? The belief in qualia is one of the strongest arguments against functionalist accounts of consciousness. In seeing how he overcomes this objection, we can come to see why dispositions are central to Dennett's account of consciousness.

Qualia, according to those who believe in them, have four characteristics. First, they are ineffable in the sense that no words can tell you what it is for me to have an experience of redness or of pain; if you do not already have these experiences yourself, no words of mine will ever be able to communicate them to you. Secondly, the qualitative aspect of a sense datum is intrinsic to it, that is, it can be found in the isolated sense datum itself without reference to anything beyond the experience, such as language, memory, or context. Thirdly, qualia are private: only I can know whether what I am experiencing is redness or pain. Finally, I have direct or immediate acquaintance with my qualia; that is, I do not need any procedures or instruments to discover which qualia are present to me: I know in some unmediated way what it is that I experience.

Consider the sonar experiences of bats, as Nagel and others have done. We know in an objective, scientific manner that bats perceive their surroundings by means of reflected sound waves, but the subjective experience of such qualia is forever unimaginable for us. We can never know "what it is like to be a bat." The intrinsic, private nature of such states means that scientific investigations of consciousness are forever doomed to failure, they think.

This scientific inaccessibility seems particularly clear in the case of color qualia, such as redness. Many philosophers have thought about the possibility that our color experiences might be reversed. Can we not imagine a possible scenario in which, perhaps for genetic reasons, I have always had the experience of redness on the occasions when what you experience is greenness, but since I have learned to call my experience "green," neither of us have noticed? Indeed, as it is set up, no one could ever know.

Maybe the difficulty here is simply one of communication, so consider an alternative thought-experiment designed to bypass this factor. In the intrapersonal version, I wake up one morning with my own spectrum of colors inverted, seeing red grass and green sunsets. Perhaps some evil neurosurgeon has operated on me during the night and switched my input circuits. I still say the same things as I did, I behave in the same way, and my other mental operations remain unchanged. Is it not obvious, suggests this intuition pump, that the phenomenal qualities of my experiences would be radically different, even though all my cognitive functions remain the same? Hence, the qualophile concludes, functionalism is inadequate as an account of consciousness.

Hold on, says Dennett, the experiment is incomplete! If the aim is to show that the qualia can change while *all* the functions remain constant, then we will need a second surgical intervention to switch the output functions as well. If, for instance, red used to make me anxious and green peaceful, our second intervention must adjust these emotions so that the red grass will now incline me to peacefulness. If the red sunset used to remind me of roses and stir patriotic memories of my nation's red flag, the second surgery must associate these memories with greenness. If my typical reaction to the greenness of the grass was to lie on it, from now on it must be the redness of the grass that inclines me to this behavior. Above all, of course, I will need my language module to be adjusted so that I will now verbally describe the "red" grass as green and the "green" sunset as red. Before the double surgery, my heterophenomenological report stated that the sunset was red and the grass green. After the surgery my report will still state that the sunset is red and the grass green. So, listening to me, you will not know that there has been any change. Note that since, by definition, a heterophenomenological report is a sincere one, I too believe that what I am experiencing is a red sunset and green grass. That is, my conscious state, in so far as I am experiencing it, seems to me to be unchanged.

The qualophiles—as Dennett calls them—mistakenly think of color experiences as intrinsically defined and as isolated, atomic entities unrelated to the rest of life. Dennett proposes that we think of such experiences as defined by the wider context of functional processes that they are a part of. The redness of a rose is related not just to perception, but to memory, emotion, symbolism, behavior and, of course, language. The fact that this context is complex makes it difficult to put it into words, which may lead people to describe it as ineffable. The difficulty is due, however, not to some mysterious feature of the mental reality itself, but to the complexity of the functions. Similarly, the so-called privacy of qualia is illusory: all that individuals have access to are the judgements made, that is, how things seem to them—the contents of their heterophenomenological reports. We have no direct access to hypothetical qualia on the Cartesian screen or elsewhere; we have only our beliefs about how things seem to be.

All conscious experiences are embedded in a complex network of dispositions; their roles in this network distinguish experiences from each other. It may seem that experiences are characterized by intrinsically defined qualia, but this is an illusion: the truth is they are characterized by their functional relationships. If by qualia we mean mental entities that are ineffable, intrinsic, private and directly accessible, then there are no such entities. Dennett wholeheartedly agrees that there *seem* to be qualia; in fact they do not exist.

But what about pain? Pain is a particularly good example of a quale, at least at first sight. It seems absolutely evident that there is something it is like to have a pain; it has a distinctive quality: it hurts. Surely the qualophile is right in this case?

The qualophile's account of pain is deceptively simple. A pain is right there in my consciousness, present in a way I have difficulty ignoring. If I put my hand on a hot stove, a sensation is sent immediately to consciousness, the sensation of pain. It has in itself a distinctive quality, so that I cannot fail to recognize it as different from pleasure or from redness. It seems self-evident that the actual experience is something other than the existence of various brain functions, for even if a computer, touching a hot stove, were to say it was in pain—even if it were to take aversive action—we could never believe that it really experienced pain. No functional analysis could ever account for the quality of pain as a conscious experience, claims the qualophile.

Dennett sets out to undermine the strength of these simple intuitions. First, on a purely physiological level, the situation is more complex than it appears at first sight. Input from the pain nerves is processed in the spinal cord. Feedback to the spine from higher cognitive functions in the brain already modifies the peripheral signals, sometimes even blocking them completely. The information may immediately trigger motor responses controlled by the spinal cord, such as initiating the withdrawal of one's hand from a hot stove, that may occur hundreds of milliseconds before any pain messages reach the brain. Arriving at the brain, these signals are integrated with information from other sensory inputs, with hormonal influences, with input from areas concerned with desire and belief and with many other parts of the brain. Only after all this processing is the pain experienced. Physiologically, the experienced sensation of pain is never the simple arrival of nerve impulses transmitted directly from the periphery.

On a psychological level, the situation is just as complex. Some people enjoy taking a hot sauna and then throwing themselves naked in the snow—a painful experience if ever there was one! Athletes may run through pain and find it exhilarating enough to do again and again. In the Lamaze method of natural childbirth, women become convinced that what they are experiencing is powerful straining in the worthwhile project of producing a baby and not the "pains" of childbirth. During the First World War medics discovered that some soldiers with serious injuries—an arm blown off—experienced no pain, perhaps because they were relieved to know that they would now be sent home out of danger of death. Patients on morphine sometimes report that their pain sensation remains, but that it does not hurt anymore. (What could that mean?) Some people find sexual pleasure by being hurt. Under anaesthesia, some bodies react to the scalpel as if in pain, although the person is unconscious. On the other hand, there has been a fear that some "anaesthetics" in the past failed to prevent pain but simply paralyzed the body and blocked memory, so that after the surgery patients would deny that they had suffered. (Is unremembered pain still painful?) According to some, if a person believes they are not in pain, their belief is privileged: it could not be contradicted, even by a neurophysiologist whose nerve-scan indicates that all the pain nerves are activated. If someone is hypnotized to believe that they are not in pain, does this mean that the pain has vanished; or is the pain still really there as a mental entity but the person simply has a mistaken belief about the fact? These paradoxical psychological phenomena suggest that the theory that pain is the presence of a distinctive quality to consciousness is simplistic.

The qualophile conceives of pain as a quality of a sense datum that would still really have this intrinsic quality there on the Cartesian screen, even if the pain quality were not recognized by the conscious subject. Yet looked at more closely, this makes no sense. Consider a thought-experiment parallel to the swapping of colors. Imagine swapping the input circuits for pain and pleasure as well as all the output functions related to them. The qualophile claims that, since qualia are not functions, it is possible that the qualia might still remain unchanged. But is this reasonable? After the swap, it is the glass of wine I used to enjoy that now leads to an experience of pain, rather than the stomping on my foot that used to do so. Nevertheless, since the output functions have also been swapped, the wine-induced pain results in a fuzzy, warm, comfortable feeling, I reach eagerly to refill the glass, I report sincerely that I am enjoying it, and my own judgement and belief in that the experience is giving me pleasure. The qualophile's intuition that the actual experience, considered in isolation, still has its own intrinsic quality of being painful is now hard to credit.

Qualophiles claim that they can imagine what it would be like to experience the quality even in the absence of the functions associated with it. Dennett thinks they cannot. They pretend they are imagining it, but if they really try to imagine such a thing, they will fail. If we subtract from pain our aversive reactions, memories of our suffering in the past, anticipations of future suffering, worries about how the pain may cripple our future projects, our anxious tensions and impulsive responses, then there is nothing left; our imagination draws a blank. What makes a pain painful is not something intrinsic to it; it is the role that the experience plays in our wider network of physiological, psychological, and even social events. Painfulness is a functional property that is contextually defined. From Dennett's point of view, it is not that pain is what it is and then we have to just deal with it; it is that how we deal with our inputs determines, secondarily, how we experience them, i.e., how they seem to us. Far from being an intrinsic quality independent of other cognitive functions, pain is defined by its functional role in the network of our dispositions.

The strange phenomenon of blindsight can lead us to a similar conclusion. Some people who have damage to the optical lobes of their brains suffer from cortical blindness. That is, although their eyes still work fine, they are unable to have any visual experience in some area—a scotoma—of their visual field. Of these patients a proportion are able when prompted to "guess" correctly about stimuli in their blind area at a rate above chance; some even guess right most of the time. Typically, when asked about the shape or movement of an object in their scotoma, they initially protest that they are blind and can see nothing. Only when a researcher insists that they guess, do they offer the verbal responses that may be surprisingly correct. This is in no way miraculous. There are a number of different pathways between the retina and the brain, so some retinal information may still be available even if that part of the cortex responsible for visual experience is damaged.

What does this mean for qualia? A Cartesian would be inclined to say that, since the information never makes it to consciousness, the blindsighted person must be responding to such information in a mechanistic or automatic manner. That is, what we have here is a case where input and output functions are intact, but consciousness is absent: there are no qualia. So once again it appears as if the functionalist approach leaves something out.

However, the experimental situation is more ambiguous than that. In fact, blindsighted people do not respond automatically to such stimuli; they do nothing until they are urged to guess. So consciousness has some role to play. If the stimulus were purely unconscious, it might well be possible to develop a conditioned reflex. Indeed in the blindsight case, people may have unconscious galvanic skin responses to stimuli in their scotoma and these may well be trainable. What we cannot do is ask the subject to raise his hand every time a light shines in his scotoma; he will simply say that he is blind and can see nothing in the area. It is as if, in blindsight, there is a disconnect between the retinal input and the reporting function, his language facility. Yet it is not a total disconnect, for when instructed to guess he may report correctly. How are we to interpret this instruction to guess? Are we telling the subject, "Whenever you are conscious of an unconscious stimulus, please tell us"? That surely is nonsense. The instruction only makes sense if the stimulus is reportable; indeed the subject's response is precisely a heterophenomenological report. The reportability, however, is flimsy, unreliable, and very thin, which is perhaps why it is not spontaneously reported. This is not surprising, since the rich channel of information, the one through the optical cortex, is the one that is damaged and unavailable. If, through training, the subject could learn to enrich the connections between the information available and their other capacities (to attend, to react, to talk) so that "guessing" became more spontaneous, then the subject would respond more like a regularly sighted person. Would they then be conscious of the stimulus? Dennett speculates that they would.

Whether he is empirically right or not is a secondary issue. What is at stake is the nature of consciousness. In opposition to the on-the-screen, intrinsic quality model of consciousness, Dennett is proposing that to say a stimulus is conscious is to say that the perceptual information is integrated with other cognitive functions, with dispositions to act in various ways, and, most notably, with the linguistic capacity to report. The importance of the linguistic or reporting function becomes particularly clear as we move to the fourth way of understanding the role of context: the zombie hunch.

"Zombie" is a philosophical, technical term of art, not to be confused with other popular uses of this term; it does not mean the sleepwalking monsters of voodoo cults. Those who speak of zombies have a hunch that there could be beings who look and act like humans, and, crucially, possess exactly the same internal cognitive functions as humans, but nevertheless lack consciousness. One might think of this as an extension of the blindsighted situation to all modalities of consciousness. Again, the target is functionalism: one can imagine all the functions being in place, but the qualia still being absent. Could we not program a computer so that it had not only all the behavioral responses to pain, but also all the internal functions associated with pain, while still not experiencing anything with a painful quality? Hence, those with the zombie hunch argue, consciousness cannot be "reduced" to any combination of cognitive functions, neural circuits, or behavioral constellations.

The argument is a contemporary version of Descartes' claim that he can conceive of mind independently of body, and so they must be separate substances. It is also related to the Turing test. Turing speculated that as computers developed there might come a time when, if we put a computer and a human behind screens, we would be unable to tell by communicating with them which was which. The notion of a zombie takes this speculation one step further by moving on from behaviorism to functionalism. It is not just that we couldn't tell the difference between a zombie and a human behaviorally; even if we had full access to all their cognitive functions, we could still not tell which had qualia, that is, which were conscious. John is a zombie; Mary is a possessor of qualia. They both make the same judgements, arrive at the same beliefs, and say the same things. No objective observer could tell the difference.

But, objects Dennett, how could a subject tell the difference either? Try to imagine the situation in detail. Step on the zombie's toe. It will say, "That hurts." It will act by withdrawing its foot. Adrenaline will flow, anger circuits will be activated, and the event will be imprinted in memory. Second-order functions, such as belief, will cut in so that the zombie will believe itself to be in pain, and say so. If you respond by insisting to the zombie that these are not real beliefs or pains because it is not conscious, it will reply (given our definition of the zombie as functionally isomorphic to a human) that it is of course conscious. We can call on the heterophenomenological method, which is designed precisely to be neutral and objective in this kind of case. The report will include not only mention of the pain, but even the claim that it believes itself to be conscious. Should you believe it? Since heterophenomenological reports are not only sincere but privileged in the sense that what the reporter says goes, you and I must believe it.

The real question, says Dennett, is whether the zombie itself believes it. Since its functions, by hypothesis, are identical to ours, it may tell itself, even silently, that it is conscious. Such a being would not be a zombie, but an ordinary, conscious person! How could I tell whether I am a zombie or not? After all, if I were a zombie, I would believe I see red; I would judge that I'm feeling pain. I would believe myself to be conscious. Can we really imagine a being that sincerely believes itself to be in pain and that believes itself to be conscious, but is neither? A being like that is unimaginable. Dennett and Descartes agree on one thing: if an entity believes itself to be conscious, then it is. The notion of a zombie is preposterous. Qualophiles claim they can imagine such beings, but in fact they cannot. A being with all the right cognitive functions would necessarily be conscious.

Zombies are proposed by their authors as a kind of reductio ad absurdum of functional accounts of consciousness. Dennett's claim is that their preposterousness demonstrates the absurdity of accounting for consciousness by appealing to a *je ne sais quoi*, to an ineffable quale. The integration of a cognitive process with other brain functions, most notably linguistic ones, is what it is for that process to be conscious.

The point of these four investigations—qualia, pain, blindsight, and zombies—is to lead us to Dennett's extrinsic account of consciousness. An entity may be what it is intrinsically, that is, because of properties of the entity itself. Alternatively, an entity may be defined extrinsically, that is, by means of relationships that it has with other entities, with its context. A piece of zinc is a piece of zinc because of the structure of its molecules, without reference to anything external. A $10 bill, on the other hand, is defined by the monetary and exchange system it is a part of. It would be a conceptual mistake to take the $10 bill to a laboratory and then declare that, since the laboratory tests can only detect its mass, size, color, chemical composition, and so on, its monetary value must be some nonphysical, mysterious, and ineffable quality.

The qualophile makes a similar mistake. He proposes an intrinsic account of consciousness: an experience is conscious if it has a specific, though ineffable, property: its quale. This is to think of consciousness as zinclike. Dennett's alternative, extrinsic view is that a process is conscious if it fits into its cognitive context in a suitable way; the analogy is with the $10 bill. An experience is conscious in so far as it is integrated in the appropriate way into a network of dispositions. To say it is conscious is to point to its functional role in the cognitive processes that make up our perceptual, motor, reflective, and linguistic capacities.

Dennett denies outright the existence of qualia. He is not simply claiming that the swapping of input and output functions modify the intrinsically defined qualia of color or of pain; he is claiming that there are no qualia in the first place. Of course, there *seem* to be; but this seeming can be accounted for by reference to the complex of dispositions related to the input. The nervous system discriminates the redness of the sunset, for instance, and these discriminations activate various emotions, memories, actions, words, beliefs, and so on. The color red itself is a complex set of reflective properties of objects in the world. The experience of being conscious of an object as red is the internal state of the organism when it has discriminated these reflective properties and has responded to them in the ways that it is predisposed to. As Dennett puts it:

> Don't our internal discriminated states *also* have some special "intrinsic" properties, the subjective, private, ineffable properties that constitute *the way things look to us* (sound to us, smell to us, etc.)? No. The dispositional properties of those discriminative states already suffice to explain *all* the effects: the effects on both peripheral behavior (saying "Red!" stepping the brake, etc.) and "internal" behavior (judging "Red!" seeing something *as* red, reacting with uneasiness or displeasure if, say, red things upset one). (BC 143)

Dennett's treatments of color and pain—and for that matter blindsight and zombies—give us the formal framework for his contextual theory of consciousness. Consciousness is not an intrinsic, but a functional property; it is a role that certain cognitive processes play within a wider network of dispositions, cognitive and behavioral. Yet which functional properties are involved? What is this network of dispositions? What context is it that defines a process as conscious? We now turn to his attempt to flesh out this framework.

MULTIPLE DRAFTS MODEL

The Multiple Drafts Model (MDM) is how Dennett labels his fleshed out theory of consciousness. We start with unconscious mechanisms. Input from the senses is initially processed and analyzed in various ways and the results broadcast widely throughout the neural system. Many circuits whose function might broadly be described as "recognizers" become activated to a greater or lesser extent and compete with each other. A visual shape sent to the optical system might initially activate a tree recognizer, but a person recognizer may also become activated and run in parallel with the tree recognition function. As more information becomes available—it's wearing clothes!—one of the circuits, say that for recognizing persons, may become even more strongly activated, while the tree recognizer loses strength. Circuits for distinguishing between men and women, friend or foe, familiar or stranger, and so on compete for levels of activation. The information is under continuous "editorial revision."

Recognizers send their results forward to other parts of the system. It is crucial to understand that what they send on is not the raw data they have received, but their conclusions or their "judgements." The given—the data—must be "taken"; they must be interpreted. It is the interpreted meaning that is forwarded to other brain centers. Dennett refers to the recognitions as "micro-takings." Recognizers are "content-fixation" devices: it is the discriminated content that they send on for other processes to deal with. Recall the analogy with Optical Character Recognition programs made in Chapter 2: what an OCR program sends on to a word processor is not the scanned shape or image of a letter, but the ASCII code that identifies the letter it has recognized. Cartesians and traditional empiricists imagine the neural system forwarding raw sensation to consciousness, which then makes one central judgement about these data. Dennett thinks this is inverted: content-fixations are like "mini-judgements" that take place early in processing; only the "conclusions" get sent on and may become conscious. The Cartesian's single unified act of interpretation must be fragmented into many micro-takings distributed in cerebral space and time. Judgement—at least some of the time— takes place before consciousness rather than after.

> . . . [N]ow we are poised for the novel feature of the Multiple Drafts model: Feature detections or discriminations *only have to be made once*. That is, once a particular "observation" of some feature had been made, by a specialized, localized portion of the brain, the information content thus fixed does not have to be sent somewhere else to be rediscriminated by some "master" discriminator. (CE 113)

Each of these cognitive processes can be thought of as a "draft" of experience. These drafts do not just sit there passively; they are active: as soon as each recognizer is stimulated, however tentatively, it activates to a greater or lesser extent other associated neural circuits involved in memory, emotion, language, or action. There is no question of waiting for the drafts to reach some definitive finish line—for them to be "finalized"—before they have various effects. The words, for instance, may already blurt out—"it's a bird, it's a plane, it's Superman!"—before any "final" recognition has occurred. One may already spring back, startled, before realizing that a looming object is only a tree, not a person. The head and eyes may turn, in an almost reflex manner, toward something that looks like a person. Memory circuits are activated by someone who looks familiar. A warm feeling is aroused when the friend recognizer becomes activated. The name of the object or person becomes activated in the linguistic areas of the brain. As the input is analyzed further, some of these associated circuits increase in activation while others will fall by the wayside. Some actions may be initiated but then quickly aborted.

This means that at any given moment there are multiple drafts competing in parallel with each other. Which of these multiple drafts is the content of consciousness? There is no definitive answer, claims Dennett. There is no "final" or "published" canonical draft that, in itself, is conscious. Rather, the multiple streams may be probed in various ways, resulting in specific heterophenomenological reports or narratives. To return to the phi phenomenon, if we probe early enough we may get a report of a single red spot; if we probe later, we get a report of a moving spot changing color. In the case of the woman wearing a hat or not, we get different answers depending when we ask. "But which version is the subject herself really conscious of?" That is exactly the question that is out of order, for it is asked from the standpoint of the Cartesian Theater. In the Multiple Drafts Model, which draft gets declared "conscious" depends on the functional context; there is no "fact of the matter."

The claim that the status of being conscious refers to the functional role of a cognitive process within a network of dispositions, while true, may leave the impression of a static role, a role within a network of simultaneous processes. Yet the functional role that Dennett is thinking of is also temporal; it is diachronic as well as synchronic. Consciousness can no more be defined at an instant that it can be defined intrinsically. The conception of consciousness as an "instantaneous flicker" is an incoherent notion. As Dennett puts it, "And then what happens?" What happens *after* an event determines retroactively the conscious status of the event.

As "realists" about consciousness, we believe that there has to be something—some property K—that distinguishes conscious events from nonconscious events. Consider the following candidate for property K: A contentful event becomes conscious if and when it *becomes part of a temporarily dominant activity in the cerebral cortex.* (BC 134)

Being conscious can be thought of as analogous to being famous; it is "fame in the brain," as he sometimes puts it. It makes no sense to refer to someone as being famous only for an hour, a minute, or a second. Part of the meaning of fame is that the status must endure for a minimum period of time—however vaguely defined. To be a celebrity for an hour and then forgotten is precisely *not* to be a celebrity. "Consciousness, like fame, is a *functionalistic* phenomenon" (SD 164). Whether an event in the brain is conscious or not depends on what happens next, on how the process is taken up by verbal, emotional, or action functions in the brain; it is its "fame" in the wider temporal context that qualifies it as conscious.

Consciousness is cerebral celebrity—nothing more and nothing less. Those contents are conscious that persevere, that monopolize resources long enough to achieve certain typical and "symptomatic" effects—on memory, on the control of behavior and so forth. (BC 137)

Mental contents become conscious not by entering some special chamber in the brain, not by being transduced into some privileged and mysterious medium, but by winning the competitions against other mental contents for domination in the control of behavior, and hence for achieving long-lasting effects—or as we misleadingly say, "entering into memory." And since we are talkers, and since talking to ourselves is one of our most influential activities, one of the most effective ways—not the only way—for a mental content to become influential is for it to get into position to drive the language-using parts of the controls. (FE 254)

LANGUAGE

Language is at the center of Dennett's notion of consciousness in a way analogous to the central role that vision plays in the Cartesian model of consciousness. In visual perception, first there is an object in the world that is there whether it is perceived or not, and then, secondarily, there is perception, which may, or may not, be faithful to the object. The Cartesian internalizes this model and conceives of consciousness as inner perception. A caricature of the model would look like this: first there is the object on the Cartesian Theater; then there is the perceiving of it, accurately or inaccurately; and finally there may be speech about the object. Dennett thinks that this perceptual model should not be taken all the way in and used to explain consciousness in the brain. The cartoon for his model is more like this: first there is the generation of the hetero-phenomenological report; within this report the world as it seems to us—the objects that we are conscious of—is generated. This caricature brings out the centrality of language in Dennett's account of consciousness.

However, if he rejects the Cartesian claim that we speak because we first see, Dennett owes us an alternative account of how language and its contents come about. The theory he is rejecting could be put this way: first there is a Central Meaner that somehow (how?) figures out what needs to be said and then sends directions to a language module that finds the appropriate words and grammatical structures that are then vocalized. What needs to be explained is something like this: "Mary figures out what she means to say and says it." Proposing that there is a mini-Mary who has already figured out what she means to say—the Central Meaning homunculus—and then gets Mary to say it, attempts to explain the generation of meaning by appealing to a meaning already generated. This mystifies rather than enlightens the process. What we need to account for is not how to translate an already composed meaning into English speech, but to explain how an initial linguistic meaning comes to be composed in the first place. If we do not do this at some level, we fall into an infinite regress.

A better model, says Dennett, is to start with a senseless vocal stream—think of a baby's babbling—that is then modulated by various factors before being released. Words should be thought of as neural structures proactively trying to modulate the stream to get themselves said. Some computer programmers who use this technique of proactive structures call them "demons." At any given moment, some of these demons will be more activated than others, due to the influence of the many competing parallel cognitive processes coming from perceptual inputs, desires, awakened memories, and so on. The result is "pandemonium," a number of parallel verbal streams—multiple "utterance drafts"—that are then filtered through various enhancing or censoring processes until a final version is released. We all have the experience of wondering what to say, of multiple possibilities on the tip of our tongues, and often, of being surprised at the outcome. While sometimes we may rehearse a piece of speech in advance, often, especially in live conversation, we do not know what we're going to say until it gets said.

Among the utterances the pandemonium process gives rise to are heterophenomenological reports. These report "how things seem to the speaker." Of the many parallel cognitive processes going on, those that succeed in influencing the language generation model in such a way that they get said are those that thereby become "conscious." Part of what it means for a process to gain fame in the brain is that it gets itself spoken in the heterophenomenological report. Language is not an incidental, secondary consequence of consciousness; language is essential to consciousness. It is not, "first I see, then I speak," but rather "because I speak about it, it seems this way to me."

We can, of course, talk to ourselves. Indeed, Dennett speculates, this might be how reflective thought originated. At some stage in our evolution, when language was being used solely to communicate with others, it might have proved useful to some early Homo Sapiens, finding herself in a tricky situation alone, to ask aloud an imaginary companion what to do next. Hearing her own question, new and different brain circuits might have been stimulated—autostimulation, as Dennett calls it—allowing her to offer aloud a solution. Ruminating to oneself out loud in this way could later have given rise to a shortcut in the brain, bypassing the peripheral elements of the vocal and hearing mechanisms and leading to silent, reflective thought. So Dennett's claim that consciousness is linked to language does not imply that it must be vocalized aloud.

But am I not the one speaking? Does this account of language generation imply that what is said is not my responsibility? This objection, once again, involves imposing a model from the physical world onto consciousness—taking things too far in. Responsibility is a global attribute. The responsibility for what gets said rests on me as one, unified person. It is my perceptions, my memories, my desires, and my personality that lead to this speech act rather than another: Dennett's account explains the mechanism of how I accomplish it. Indeed the account he is rejecting could be accused of stripping me of my responsibility and assigning it to some internal homunculus, a mini-Mary or Central Meaner, rather than to me as a full-fledged, individual person. Once again, the error is due to taking a model appropriate to the global level and applying it to the components. As a global person, I am responsible for what I say. The buck stops here.

THE STREAM OF CONSCIOUSNESS

Dennett's account of language is crucial for understanding consciousness. The mechanics of the production of language can be explained by neural processes within the brain; but what gets said, the content or the meaning of the language, is the responsibility of the whole individual. In so far as the final production is a (hetero-phenomenological) report, it is an account of how things seem to me, the global individual who is conscious. There is a conceptual divide between the underlying material processes and the content of language and consciousness. When Conan Doyle writes a novel about Sherlock Holmes and his adventures, Holmes cannot be found on the physical page. On the page there is only ink; Holmes is in London. The vehicle of the story and the content of the story are very different things. It would be a mistake to think of Holmes' adventures as a second, ghostly process hovering over the physical process of the ink on the paper. The difference is much more radical than that. It is the difference between the vehicle of expression—the process of representing—and the meaning or content expressed—the represented. Consciousness is of the order of the content, not of the vehicle. Consciousness is virtual with respect to the reality of neural processes.

The virtual nature of consciousness can be brought out by looking at, first, the "stream" of consciousness and, secondly, Dennett's claim that consciousness is "gappy."

Consciousness seems to us to flow by as a single sequence, the kind vividly exemplified by James Joyce and other "stream of consciousness" authors. An iceberg may appear to track against the wind; this is because the much larger mass of the iceberg under the water is propelled by ocean currents. By analogy, on the surface, conscious experiences seem to flow in a single continuous stream; under the surface, in the reality of the brain, there are massively parallel structures with multiple information processes going on simultaneously. Many of these processes die out within a few hundred milliseconds; others may persist longer, but very few "make it to consciousness," that is, get to be heterophenomenologically reported in a single, sequential, Joycean stream. Dennett refers to the sequential Joycean stream as like a virtual program emulated by the parallel processes of the brain. Just as the Windows operating system can be run virtually on a Linux-operated computer, so the sequential nature of consciousness can be thought of as a virtual process—the user interface, as one might put it.

The virtual interface makes the stream of consciousness seem continuous, a plenum stretched out before us both in space and in time. In reality, consciousness is very "gappy." There is a blind spot on the retina that we receive no information from—a spatial gap. The eye darts around the visual field in saccades and during its rapid movements the information feed is interrupted—a temporal gap. Yet we have no awareness of these gaps. We cannot identify the color of a playing card in our peripheral vision, nor are we always aware of major changes in front of our eyes (as explained in Chapter 2 above). Yet we *seem* to be conscious of these things. The continuity is virtual; it is in the content of consciousness, which must therefore be clearly distinguished from the neural, informational processes.

The point of these considerations is to bring out the virtual nature of consciousness. What is really going on in the brain, the cognitive functions implemented by the neural circuits, must not be confused with how things seem to the subject, that is, with consciousness. The brain involves parallel processes, gappy information flow, events on the millisecond time scale, while consciousness is a continuous, uninterrupted, sequential stream, without gaps, on an experiential time scale.

The virtual nature of consciousness becomes particularly evident when we consider prosthetic vision. If a person with retinal blindness has video cameras mounted on their glasses and the output converted into electrical signals that create tingling sensations on a matrix of electrical stimulators placed on their belly, they can, with practice, learn to "see" through the video cameras. They can, for instance, recognize an object as a human face. After training, their initial tingling on the belly becomes an experience that they report to be more or less like seeing; it *seems* to them like seeing. A fist looming toward the face leads to a protective reflex movement of the head, not a movement of the belly where the signals are really being received. One can call this vision "virtual," since, although the real neural sensations actually occur on the belly, the person seems to have visual experiences of faces, fists, and other objects from the perspective of the head. "Virtuality" refers to the fact that how things seem may not be how they really are. Note that, if we use the term this way, ordinary seeing, with a regular, intact retina, is also virtual: we have no experience of retinal sense data— the things that are "really" going on—but rather seem to be seeing objects in the world. In other words, all consciousness is virtual. How we experience things is how they seem to us.

Dennett complains that some Americans, traveling in countries foreign to them, consider local currencies to be "funny" money, to be invalid or virtual, and ask, "How much is that in real money?" But all money is a social construct; all money is virtual in contrast with the reality of paper bills or metal coins. Analogously, all consciousness is virtual in the sense that it is of a quite different order than neural or physical processes, even when these processes underlie and enable experience. Visual experience is virtual with respect to either belly tactile sensations or retinal firings; Holmes is virtual with respect to the ink on Doyle's pages; the Joycean stream of consciousness is virtual with respect to the multiply parallel processes of the brain.

IS CONSCIOUSNESS AN ILLUSION?

So ultimately, Dennett, is consciousness real or is it an illusion? Is your claim that it is virtual not a way of sitting on the fence? Is your theory of consciousness not all about seeming rather than about what is true?

The question itself is part of the problem. The terms "seem" and "illusion" are used in a number of ways. In one sense, "illusory" just means "false." When we say, "John's apparent success was an illusion," we imply that it is false that he was successful. Yet Dennett is not claiming that "there is consciousness" is false. He sits on his rocker on his front porch and takes time to smell the roses. He is aware of and enjoys the redness of the flowers and the richness of the world he is perceiving. He is on, he assures us, not off his rocker. He believes in the existence of consciousness as much as the rest of us. His project is to explain consciousness, not to explain it away.

Indeed, Dennett's heterophenomenological method gives the existence of consciousness a privileged status. We need to suspend judgement, of course, on whether my experience is true of the world—what Husserl calls the phenomenological reduction—but the report of how it seems to the speaker is unchallengeable. In Dennett's method there is no room for the possibility that consciousness itself is an illusion nor that we could be deluded about the content of consciousness, about how things seem to us.

Nevertheless, there is an illusion in the vicinity. Sticking with how things seem to us is far from easy. The difficult part of the heterophenomenological method is abstaining from judgements about reality, about how things really are. The temptation is to do as we normally do in everyday reports and assume that what is reported truly is real. A speaker may report hearing voices and claim that they are caused by Satan, who must be inhabiting his head. There is no Satan in the head. That is an illusion. We must take the heterophenomenological report that the speaker seems to hear voices as sacrosanct, but the speaker's theory about the cause of this experience—Satan—slips over into making judgements about reality. The fact that the purported reality referred to is in the head does not mean that it shares in the privileged certainty the reporter has about how things seem to him. In the heterophenomenological method we are to abstract from *all* reality. The speaker has absolute authority over how things seem to him; he has no special authority over the real cause, mental or physical, that any theory uses to explain why things seem that way. Centuries of Cartesian indoctrination have made the theory that there are real mental representations causing our experience seem like common sense. These are the theoretical mental entities that Dennett is claiming are illusory.

Yet the term "seem" is often used in a different sense, not to mean false, but to distinguish between appearance and reality, to distinguish how things are in experience from how they are in themselves. The table *seems to me* to be solid, though physics tells me *it is really* mostly empty space. Descartes' distant tower seems small, though in reality it is big. The rose seems red, though the reality is that it reflects certain wavelengths of light. The pin poked in my finger feels painful, though it is really just sharp. In these cases we are not talking about the difference between truth and falsity, but between how things actually are and how they appear to us. "The rose seems red," in this sense, does not imply that anything is false; the statement just focuses on the way that light waves of a certain kind are experienced as opposed to how they are physically, how they are "in-themselves."

The content of consciousness is the realm of appearance, of how things seem. It is not the realm of reality. The smallness of the tower and the painfulness of the pin are not real. So there is one sense in which we can say consciousness is not real. It would be a mistake to conclude, however, that this means it is illusory in the other sense, that is, to conclude that it is false that there is consciousness.

So Dennett holds that it is true that there is consciousness. He objects, however, to taking the appearance-reality dichotomy and applying it within consciousness itself. Consciousness is pure seeming. The Cartesian mistake is to take the appearance-reality distinction all the way in. The distinction is perfectly valid to describe the relationship between the mind and the world; it has no place *within* the mind. Consciousness is how things seem to us; it is meaningless to distinguish between how things *really* seem to us and how things *seem* to seem to us. "There is no such phenomenon as really seeming—over and above the phenomenon of judging in one way or another that something is the case" (CE 364). The notion of how things really seem to us posits a "seeming" as a kind of in-itself, a reality that has its own intrinsic properties independent of how we are conscious of it. As we saw in Chapter 2, it is this notion of "real seemings," of mental, in-itself reality that Dennett rejects as an illusion. Consciousness itself is not an illusion.

> The familiar ideas die hard. It seemed obvious to many that consciousness is—must be—rather like an inner light shining, or rather like television, or rather like a play or movie presented in the Cartesian Theater. If they are right, then consciousness would have to have certain features that I deny it to have. But they are simply wrong. When I point this out I am not denying the reality of consciousness at all; I am just denying that consciousness, real consciousness, is like what they think it is like. (BC 139)

* * *

Rejecting both the eliminativist position that there is no consciousness—that consciousness is pure illusion—and the Cartesian notion of consciousness as the presence of intrinsically defined mental entities to a homunculus, Dennett explains consciousness in terms of functional and dispositional context. According to his MDM, there are many parallel cognitive functions in the brain that give rise to multiple drafts of experience. Which draft becomes conscious depends on the context and, especially, the context of language generation, of the production of the heterophenomenological report. The result is the sequence that makes up the stream of consciousness. This sequence is virtual in the sense that it cannot be identified with neural realities.

Dennett's theory of consciousness is the foundation for his account of the evolution of narrative selfhood, but before we can discuss the nature of the self in Chapter 5, we must first master his novel interpretation of evolution.

CHAPTER 4

EVOLUTION: GETTING HERE FROM THERE

Dennett's explanation of consciousness, as we have seen, shows in principle how mind can be embedded in the physical processes of the brain without being simply reduced to them. There is a major lacuna, however, in the account so far: Why is there mind in the first place?

Darwin has pointed the way toward an answer: evolution by natural selection. Dennett takes what he calls "Darwin's Dangerous Idea" and elaborates it into a full-fledged, naturalistic method that allows him to explain the origin of biological function, language, meaning, and selfhood within the biological and physical world. Once again, Dennett steers carefully between accounts that reduce human life to the purely biological and otherworldly appeals to the supernatural. Static and essentialist views of human nature give way to historical and contingent accounts of human emergence that preserve the uniqueness of human existence while still explaining its origin through evolution.

We will first examine Darwin's theory and Dennett's elaboration of it. Then we will discuss how the elaborated theory can account for the emergence of intentionality, reason, and mind.

DARWIN'S THEORY OF EVOLUTION

Darwin's idea is deceptively simple. Any life form will naturally tend to reproduce at an exponential rate, a fact Darwin learned from Malthus. For example, a bacterium will produce two offspring that, in the next generation, will produce four. The subsequent generation will have eight and, in general the xth generation will have 2^x members. In a surprisingly short time, the bacterium would cover the whole world. This mathematical tendency to exponential growth is a fundamental feature of any reproducing life form.

In principle, the characteristics of the reproducing parent are inherited by the offspring. In practice, no two biological individuals are exactly alike, and some of this variety can be passed on to descendants. In an environment constrained by limiting factors such as nutrition, space, and other organisms, some of these variations will give the offspring and its descendants an advantage or disadvantage in the competition for survival and reproduction. Even a very minor advantage, given the exponential nature of growth, can have an enormous effect after many generations. Well-adapted, or "fit," individuals will have more descendants than their less adapted competitors. The result will be a gradual change in the population: traits that help an organism survive and reproduce will accumulate over generations. Species will therefore change their characteristics over time. This is the principle of adaptation or "survival of the fittest."

Darwin refers to the process as "natural selection," by analogy with artificial selection. Breeders, consciously or unconsciously, have for millennia selected variants in plants or animals for the breeders' advantage. Nature has, in an analogous fashion, gradually and cumulatively selected traits on the basis of fitness for survival; this process explains the emergence of the species extant today. The process is automatic in the sense that, unlike breeders, nature has no goal, either conscious or unconscious.

Darwin's scheme, as people at the time quickly saw, offers a naturalistic explanation for the evident fact that organisms are well designed for their environment. No longer is there any need to appeal to God as an Intelligent Designer, to call upon any mysterious *élan vital*, or to anthropomorphize Mother Nature as an entity with conscious purposes. It is not that nature "sets out" to "select" the fittest—that would be artificial selection. It is simply that the fittest survive and replicate while the less fit die off.

Since Darwin's time, we have learned that all cells have a set of genes made up of DNA, its genotype, that determine the characteristics of the individual organism, the phenotype. The genes are passed on during reproduction, which accounts for the conservation of traits over generations, and they occasionally undergo mutations, which accounts for the variations in the phenotype.

59

THE ADAPTATIONIST ALGORITHM

As Dennett interprets him, Darwin makes two independent claims. The first claim is that the contemporary range of species can be accounted for by the process of descent with modification. From some common ancestor, a continual series of changes explains the set of species currently visible. His second, more novel, claim is that this process of descent operates by the mechanism of natural selection. As Dennett interprets and elaborates it, natural selection— adaptation—is an algorithmic process that, properly understood, can be applied much more widely than Darwin thought; indeed, it is a kind of universal acid that can dissolve almost any problem it touches. As a theory of design in general, it goes beyond biological design and can account for the origin of mind, language, meaning, and many social phenomena. Even ethics and religion are not beyond its reach. Before examining these, we must look at the notions of algorithm and design.

"Algorithm" refers to a set of instructions that can be applied to a problem mechanically, that is, without insight. The term comes from computer science, where it designates a program that can proceed automatically, step-by-step, on whatever input data it is given. The technique we all learned in school for doing long division is a case of an algorithm: whatever numbers we are given, we just apply the procedure, and the answer pops out. An algorithm for playing tic-tac-toe could proceed by listing and evaluating each of the possible sequences of moves—more than 362,000—and selecting only those that would allow you to win. Applying this procedure would guarantee that you would never again lose at tic-tac-toe!

Chess is a different matter. It is not different in principle, for again one could list all possible outcomes and choose a winning one. But it is different in practice, for the number of possible games of chess is so large that no conceivable computer, using this kind of algorithm, could hope to figure out the next move before the end of the universe. In fact, real chess computers don't even try to evaluate all possible future moves, but rely on practical procedures that use rough-and-ready methods to generate a move within the time constraints of the clock. These are called "heuristic" methods. Heuristic algorithms produce an answer for practical purposes but they are risky, for the answer is not guaranteed to be right. Their advantage is that they do produce *some* answer—the best within the constraints—while the "perfect" algorithm may still be computing when the world ends!

A tennis tournament is an example of a heuristic algorithm. It takes a number of tennis players, plays them against each other in quarter finals, semifinals, and finals and guarantees one single "winner." While it is often the case that the winner is the most skilled at tennis, this is not inevitably the case. A coin-tossing tournament also produces a single winner, though there is no skill involved, only pure luck, pure chance. Many algorithms are based on a combination of skill and chance—imagine a tennis tournament played on a very bumpy court. Even in tournaments that combine skill and chance, skill nevertheless tends to win out in the long run. Algorithms that select winners, at least partly, on the basis of skill allow us to predict the future potential of the winner. The one who wins a coin-tossing tournament, even though her coin may have come up heads 10 times in a row, has no additional likelihood of throwing heads on the next toss. In a skill-testing tournament like tennis, on the other hand, we can with some reliability predict that the player would win again.

Dennett proposes that we think of evolution as an algorithm that is partly skill-based. If a particular trait helps an organism to survive, the probability is greater than chance that the same trait, inherited by its descendants, will also improve their chances of survival. It is this algorithm that explains, in retrospect, which species exist today, the current set of winners. What the adaptationist algorithm does not do is predestine any particular trait or phenotype in advance. A tennis tournament does not have any predetermined winner in mind; it just picks out the winner, whoever that might be. For instance, it does not predetermine that the player with the best backhand wins. Similarly, in evolution, it is not the case that, say, the largest organisms automatically win: it depends on how things work out—ants have survived as well as elephants. Grass and whales are among the current winners of the evolutionary tournament, but these could not originally have been predicted. Such species or features are not among the "goals" of evolution; it has no goals in this sense. The algorithm is an automatic procedure that picks out the fittest, but it has no preconception of what the fittest traits or organisms may turn out to be. In particular, the algorithm is not aimed at the ultimate production of the human species. It is easy, in a kind of narcissistic way, to think of ourselves as the apex of evolution, as what it tended toward from the beginning. This would be a mistake. The algorithm is a blind mechanism. Human existence is a contingent development, not a predetermined goal.

The only thing the evolutionary algorithm is guaranteed to deliver is design: it produces organisms that are "fit" for their environment, i.e., that are well designed. Dennett rejects the idea that we can explain design by appealing to a pre-existing Design (the Platonic option) or a conscious Designer (the theistic option). He describes such explanations as "skyhooks,"—devices hanging from the sky with no visible means of support that still do the heavy lifting in design space. If we are to explain how design comes to be in the first place, we get nowhere by assuming that design already exists. Design and designers are what need to be explained; minds are products of evolution, not (at least initially) producers of it. The Darwinian, algorithmic approach is the only one that is not question-begging.

Nevertheless, it would be hard to credit the exquisite designs of the natural world simply to a linear sequence of conserved mutations. Instead of a sequence of one-off changes, we need to think of evolution as cumulative. By cumulative, Dennett means not just that mutant traits that enhance survival get added on to the line's heritage; it is that some mutations act as accelerators for future evolutionary moves. Natural selection in its raw form is like a wedge that raises evolution by the tiniest possible steps. Accelerators—"cranes" as opposed to wedges—speed up evolution and, just as a small construction crane can be used to set up a big crane, a cascade of cranes built on each other explains the spectacular, apparently miraculous development of design.

Sex, for example, is a magnificent crane. Compared with asexual reproduction, the combination of genetic information from two parents gives evolution a "leg up." It is easier and faster for organisms that reproduce sexually to adapt. Later, the development of language dramatically speeded up the replication of fitness traits compared to genetic inheritance. Yet unlike skyhooks, cranes are built firmly on the ground in the sense that, although the crane may explain the acceleration of evolutionary developments, it is not a miraculous skyhook: it itself can be explained as a product of evolution.

There is no need for miracles. The blind algorithm, enriched by the cranes it has itself constructed, can account for the exquisitely designed natural world without any need to appeal to pre-existing design either in the mind of an Intelligent Designer, or in the form of pre-existing forms or essences.

The idea that the design of an organism is based on a pre-existing and fixed essence is one of the most central concepts dissolved by the universal acid of Darwin's algorithm. Since Plato and Aristotle, we have understood the world in terms of eternal forms or essences. This is particularly true in biology. According to essentialism, each species is defined by distinctive and stable norms that distinguish it sharply from other species and that remain constant over time. In this respect, the title of Darwin's most influential book, *The Origin of Species*, is misleading. What the book actually does, claims Dennett, is overthrow the very notion of species itself.

Take an example. Part of the traditional essence "mammal" is having a mammal for a mother. So there can never be a first mammal! Individual mammals may come into existence, but the essence of being a mammal could never come to be; there must always have been mammals, as Aristotle seems to have maintained. Darwin's adaptationism undermines this way of thinking. Species evolve gradually; the notion that each is defined by an essence is an illusion created by taking a snapshot at one moment in time and ignoring the history of evolution. From the viewpoint of adaptationism, lines of organisms—clades—gradually developed traits that we now identify with being a mammal. We could of course arbitrarily identify one of these organisms as the First Mammal (in which case its mother would not be a mammal), but a move like this would serve more to obscure than to enlighten us about what is going on.

We can apply this thinking to the question of the first human. If we examine the DNA in the mitochondria of current human cells, we can track them back along the female line to the latest common ancestor, "mitochondrial Eve." Is she not the first member of the human species? No. It is quite possible that Eve's mother had identical DNA and so was just as much a human being, but that either all of Eve's sisters failed to reproduce or their line of descendants became extinct at some later date. It is even logically possible that, if Eve had two daughters and the descendants of one of the daughters were to die out this current year, then the other daughter would become the latest common ancestor and so, millions of years later, wrest the title of mitochondrial Eve from her mother. Which woman counts as Eve is a purely contingent matter that depends on future events, not on Eve's own characteristics. Adaptationism makes the boundaries defining the human species an arbitrary and contingent matter.

The same is true of any species. Warm-blooded creatures evolved from cold-blooded ones, but the change is not abrupt. Between them were animals who maintained a temperature only slightly above that of their environment, and other animals who maintained a homeostatic temperature for only part of the year. Such intermediate steps cannot be classified as either cold- or warm-blooded. The sharp temporal boundaries essentialism requires between species are illusions created by our everyday perspective that lacks historical depth.

Spatial boundaries are just as arbitrary. Dennett points to the case of herring gulls, who live in a broad ring around the North Pole. As we go westward from Britain, these gulls gradually undergo varietal change, though neighboring varieties can continue to interbreed—i.e., they remain members of the same "species." Nonetheless, as we complete the circle around Alaska and Siberia back toward Europe, the varietal changes have accumulated to the point where the birds qualify as lesser black-backed gulls, who although they live alongside herring gulls do not interbreed with them, and so qualify as a distinct "species." We cannot at any point around the circle simply draw an arbitrary spatial boundary separating the two species of gulls, since across any such line individual birds interbreed.

In Dennett's interpretation, then, Darwin's book, far from explaining the origin of species, shows that the notion of species cannot be defined by an intrinsic essence, by a set of essential traits. It is our pragmatic context at a particular place and time that makes it useful for us to think in terms of a "species." Nature itself must be seen as a continuum of organisms that vary gradually in space and time. It follows that intermediate stages that don't fit into our categories are to be expected. It is not only that it makes no sense to ask which organism was the first mammal; we cannot say when vision, language, or mind first originated. The problem is not that we lack the empirical evidence; gradualism means that the beginning of a trait is a contextual matter that can never be precisely defined for reasons of principle.

Gradualism also means that there must be a series of steps from the past to the present. (*Gradus* is Latin for step.) Of course, we seldom know what precisely these steps were. We do not know exactly how dinosaurs developed wings and became birds. Often, the best we can offer are what Dennett calls "Just So" stories—speculative imaginings of what the steps might possibly have been. A Just So story is not a piece of armchair science; its function is to overcome our naïve reaction that one could never get here from there—that it is unimaginable for dinosaurs, for instance, to evolve into birds. The goal of these stories is not to tell us what happened, but to show what is possible. What Dennett's gradualism excludes is the existence of species or traits that no series of possible gradual steps could ever have accessed. A theory about the structure of language that requires that the whole structure came into being in one fell swoop would therefore have to be rejected. A theory that the mind is an immaterial entity leaves no place for intermediate, partial minds, so it must be mistaken in principle. Once upon a time there were no minds. Now there are. We must be able to get from the first state to the second. Aristotle's theory that each species has its own essence allows no place for gradual, intermediate steps between species and so is inconsistent with evolution. As Dennett puts it:

> Once upon a time, there was no mind, and no meaning, and no error, and no function, and no reasons, and no life. Now all these wonderful things exist. It has to be possible to tell the story of how they all came to exist, and that story must pass, by subtle increments, from elements that manifestly lack the marvelous properties to elements that manifestly have them. There will have to be isthmuses of dubious or controversial or just plain unclassifiable intermediates. All these wonderful properties must have come into existence gradually, by steps that are barely discernible *even in retrospect.* . . .

Here is the most general form of the schema of Darwinian explanation. The task of getting from the early time when there wasn't any x to the later time when there is lots of x is completed by a finite series of steps in which it becomes less and less clear that "there still isn't any x here, not really," through a series of "debatable" steps until we eventually find ourselves on steps where it is really quite obvious that "of course there is x, lots of x." We never cross any lines. (DDI 200)

EXPLAINING BY CONTINGENCY

The gradual, stepwise approach enables us to explain why things are the way they are. "Whenever Darwinism is the topic . . . one of the precious things which is at stake is a vision of what it means to ask, and answer, the question 'Why?'" (DDI 21). The task of science is to explain why things are actually one way rather than any of the other possible ways they could be. What is a "possible way"? There are many kinds of possibility: A situation is *logically possible* if it is not self-contradictory, but many logically possible situations are not *physically possible* because they are not allowed by the laws of physics. *Biological possibility* refers to compatibility with the laws of biology but unlike logical and physical possibility, biological possibility is historical and contingent; it varies from one historical moment to the next. Thus, a giraffe with green stripes may be currently biologically impossible even though there are no logical or physical impediments to this kind of animal. Dennett defines a biological possibility as a genome or phenotype that is accessible from the current state of evolution. Six-legged animals are physically possible: ants have six legs. Nonetheless, given what mammals have become over hundreds of millions of years, a six-legged mammal is no longer a possibility. At least, it is highly improbable as the next step in gradual, evolutionary adaptation.

In biological history, then, possibility joins forces with probability. What needs to be explained in each case is not why one state occurs rather than any of the other vast number of states that are possible "in principle," but rather why, given the current state of play, the next step goes one way rather than another. For an analogy, consider the layout of computer keyboards. The QWERTY layout likely developed in early mechanical typewriters to reduce jamming the keys. While such mechanical constraints no longer govern the layout of electronic keyboards, the inertia of history makes it very improbable that we can move to a new layout. There is, if you like, a local "law of keyboards" that governs how keyboards can now be. In a similar way, there is a local biological "law of mammals" that dictates the practical impossibility of six-legged mammals. Biological laws are local restrictions due to evolutionary history. They are QWERTY-type local regularities in our biosphere.

Biological laws, then, should be seen as access possibilities in historically developed design space rather than as eternal principles like the laws of physics. There is no eternal law that the nature or essence of mammals requires that they have four legs. It is a contingent matter: the way things turned out in evolution is such that six-legged mammals are no longer accessible by the stepwise processes of adaptation. This biological necessity is described by Dennett as

> . . . "a virtual necessity," a necessity for all practical purposes, given the cards that have been dealt. . . . This marriage of chance and necessity is a hallmark of biological regularities. . . . [It] is the necessity of *reason*. It is an inescapably teleological variety of necessity, the dictate of what Aristotle called *practical reasoning*. . . . (DDI 129)

The same, of course, must be said for human "nature." There is not—against Plato and Aristotle—a form or essence of humanity that all humans possess, imitate, or participate in. To understand human minds, culture, meaning, purpose, value, and so on is not to explain them by some eternal principles or laws, but rather to QWERTY-explain them as contingent, biologically evolved regularities. So how can we apply the antiessentialist, gradualist approach to human nature?

HUMAN NATURE

Humans have a distinct nature. We have a unique value which transcends that of other animals and the physical world. Humans are rational animals: we act on the basis of reasons rather than being biologically or culturally determined. We live on the level of significance: unlike mindless mechanisms, the world is meaningful for us. In the 19th century some believed they could only defend human dignity by combatting Darwinism and denying that humankind is descended from the apes. Dennett too wants to defend the dignity of human nature, but he thinks it can be best done within the parameters of the evolutionary approach. Yes, we are conscious; yes, we have meaning in our lives; yes, we are creatures with reason; yes, we have ethical and other values. Yet we can maintain this dignity without severing our relationship with nature, without denying the integrative worldview that evolutionary science offers us. Meaning and reason fit into the evolutionary scheme. But how? We will look at meaning first.

"Intentionality" is a technical philosophical term for meaningfulness. It is often misunderstood to refer to intentional action, in the sense of deliberate action: some of my actions are said to be intentional—if I do them purposely—other actions done by accident are said to be unintentional. This is *not* the use of the term we are looking for here. We will be using intentionality to refer to "aboutness." A rock is not about anything, but the word "chair" means the object chair; the word "chair" has intentionality, while the rock has none. In an analogous way, when I am looking at a chair, my perceptual state has intentionality; it is about the chair: the chair is its meaning.

A perceptual state or word that is about a chair could be triggered by a horse; that would be a mistake. Note that a rock, in itself, cannot be a mistake. It just is. An intentional state has a norm—there is something it is supposed to be about—and since the state can fail to achieve that norm, the possibility of error is a distinctive feature of intentional states.

Some philosophers believe we must defend human dignity by maintaining that intentionality is unique to human consciousness. Only a conscious mind can mean anything. Since this seems to imply, implausibly, that words and instruments have no meaning, they distinguish between primary or original intentionality and secondary or derived intentionality. Thus, they would say that the ink that makes up the word "chair" has no intrinsic aboutness of its own: it derives its intentionality entirely from the conscious state of a person who is using that ink to mean the object chair. The intentionality of a conscious subject gives us real meaning; the ink on the paper doesn't "really" mean anything in itself. Only minds have the intrinsic properties that allow it to have a real meaning; physical things are, in themselves, intrinsically incapable of intentionality. All secondary intentionality derives from consciousness, so before the arrival of consciousness on the scene, there was no intentionality whatsoever. Such black-and-white thinking allows no room for evolutionary gradualism.

Dennett rejects this approach to intentionality as a kind of human-centered mistake. The approach is mistaken in four ways, which we will look at in turn: intentionality is not an intrinsic property, but is contextual; it is not the exclusive privilege of consciousness, for it can be found in organisms and machines; it cannot be neatly distinguished into original and derived; and it is not an all-or-nothing phenomenon.

That intentionality is not an intrinsic property is demonstrated by Dennett's "two-bitser" scenario. A soft drink vending machine designed to accept a US 25 cent piece—"two bits" in some American dialects—he labels a "two-bitser." When a US quarter is inserted, it responds by going into a state Q "which 'means' (note the scare-quotes) 'I perceive/accept a genuine US quarter now'" (DDI 404). Of course it might make a mistake: a counterfeit slug might also cause it to go into state Q—a case of "misperception." The mistake is not a causal issue; the machine has violated no causal laws. That it can be mistaken indicates that Q is an intentional state: Q means US quarter. Or does it? It happens that Panamanian quarter-balboas are, except for the writing on them, almost identical to US quarters, so in the United States they can be used as counterfeit slugs. Now let us move one of these machines to Panama where quarter-balboas are legal tender. If the machines are regularly used in Panama, state Q will come to "mean" "I have accepted a quarter-balboa," and inserting a US quarter will put it into a "mistaken" state. It is crucial to notice that nothing intrinsic has changed: the internal mechanism of the machine is identical to how it was before the move. The change in meaning is due to the context. Intentionality is not an intrinsic property of a state, but a contextual one.

"But," says our objector, "the two-bitser is a paradigmatic case of derived intentionality: what state Q means is what its designer had in mind in creating it." This objection must be wrong: the fact that in Panama Q means quarter-balboa shows that the new context overrides the meaning the original designer had in mind. "Maybe," concedes our objector, "but the new meaning is still dependent on conscious subjects, namely the new Panamanian users." Since Dennett's aim is to show that intentionality is not the exclusive privilege of any consciousness—designer or user—he must appeal to a new scenario, one with no recourse to consciousness: a frog's vision.

In the wild, a frog's eye detects flies, which the frog then catches with its tongue. This is clearly a case of intentionality, for when the catching is triggered by a piece of dirt flying by on the wind, this counts as a mistake. That the state of the frog's visual system means "fly" is due to evolutionary selection: frogs without this system tended to die out. If, in captivity, zookeepers were to launch little food pellets past the frogs, that then thrive by zapping their tongues for these pellets, would the perceptual state of the frogs still—mistakenly—mean "fly"? Would we say the same about frogs who, after many generations in captivity, have never caught a fly, only pellets? At some point—but not at a sharp boundary—we would have to say that their perceptual state would be one of pellet detection. This is a clear case of "exaptation": a mechanism originally selected for one function gets reselected for a quite different one. Despite the existence of a zookeeper in our particular scenario, there is actually no need for consciousness in this process: most exaptations are due to natural selection. While it might make some sense to distinguish original from derived intentionality in the two-bitser case, in the frog scenario the distinction makes no sense. There is no black-and-white dichotomy here between "real" intentionality—that of a conscious subject—and the derived intentionality of an instrument. Nature is opportunistic: The frog's intentional states have evolved slowly over aeons with many exaptations, but neither the earlier nor the later states derive their meaning from consciousness. Rather what we have is a contrast between early situations best described causally and those most fruitfully approached by attributing intentionality.

Even this contrast is not all-or-nothing, but a matter of degree. When we are dealing with conscious intentionality, there is a dichotomy between what is meaningful and meaningless. In nature, on the other hand, intentionality appears gradually in evolution and we can expect intermediate cases in which there is no fact of the matter about whether a trait is intentional or not. Humans often—though not always—operate with explicit, conscious meanings; but to understand the origin of this capacity we must avoid either anthropomorphizing the past or totally denying intentionality to organisms without reflective consciousness. Meaning, that is, intentionality, arrives on the evolutionary scene gradually. Does a glucose receptor on the membrane of an early bacterium "perceive food?" Is its activated state "about" sugar? Does the state "mean" or refer to the object in the world that provoked it? Or are these processes purely causal? The principle of gradualism tells us that there is no straightforward answer to any of these questions. They are intermediate stages in the development from a purely causal world to a world where there is unambiguous intentionality. We could speak of pseudo-meanings or as-if intentionality, but such labels would tell us no more than we already know.

The claim that the information processing in the frog's eye (or the meaning of state Q in the two-bitser) has a determinate meaning in itself—something it *really* means—is essence-mongering. Intentionality depends on the context of selection and changes gradually as a result of the selection process. Once we renounce essentialist thinking, we no longer need to insist that there is a right or wrong answer to whether something qualifies as a meaning. The only option for those who think in all-or-nothing terms is to conceive of meaning as given once and for all by a conscious designer. Dennett's alternative is for meaning to develop gradually through selective pressures in evolution. The rigid distinction between original and derived intentionality is therefore spurious. And he is not just speaking of frogs: the internal states of humans are just one more case of processes whose meaning is derived from what they were selected for in the process of evolution. Our meanings are just as much "derivative" as those of any other organism.

The evolution of reasons is treated by Dennett in a way analogous to the evolution of meanings.

To give a reason for something is to explain it. Aristotle held that there are four ways to explain things, but Dennett focuses on just two: causes and reasons. Why do dandelions grow fluffy white balls? One answer is that certain hormones result in the production of various proteins, etc. This is to give a cause, that is, some antecedent object or event that brings about the effect. Yet we could also answer that the fluffy balls are a good way to spread seeds in the wind. This is to give a reason, that is, the goal or purpose—that for which the event comes about. Why do spiders spin webs? The reason is to catch flies. For the cause of web-spinning, we would have to look for biochemical and genetic factors. There are hormonal causes for my heart beating faster when I run, but the reason is to supply energy to my muscles. Reasons and causes are two different modes of explanation.

While Aristotle was happy with the existence of different modes of explanation, since the birth of modern science, philosophers have found the idea problematic. Many have held that there is no place for teleological explanation—explanation by reasons—in a scientific account of the physical world: such an account should be strictly causal. While physicalists eschew explanation by reasons altogether, others compromise by treating reasons as mental causes. Dennett disagrees with both positions. Both make the same mistake: they think there is only one kind of explanation, the causal kind. Hence either they treat reasons as causes that pre-exist as purposes in the mind or else they reject all explanation by reasons as illusory.

Dennett, in opposition, sides with Aristotle in holding that "spiders spin webs to catch flies," is a valid scientific explanation—indeed an insightful one. Yet this does not mean that each spider has a pre-existing mental purpose: that would be anthropomorphism. Even if you are willing to attribute minds to spiders, it would be ludicrous to suggest that a dandelion has a purpose in mind for its fluffy seeds. The dandelion has no mind to represent the reason for its behavior. It remains the case that there is a reason for its behavior. A nonrepresented reason of this kind Dennett calls a "free-floating rationale."

To say of a trait that it has a free-floating rationale is to say that it has been designed by nature to accomplish some purpose or other. Spreading seeds is the rationale for the dandelion's fluffy balls in the sense that the balls are an adaptation to the environment that enables this variety of plant to survive. Dennett is not claiming that evolution itself has a purpose or *telos*. Quite the contrary: what he is claiming is that the adaptationist algorithm—itself without a goal—gives rise to designed organisms, that is, organisms with traits that have a free-floating rationale.

Such rationales are to be found everywhere in the biological world. Some organisms, however, have developed the ability to represent rationales, a strategy that enables a major change in evolution. Language makes it possible for humans to talk about, and so think and deliberate about, the rationales for some of their behaviors. When we do this, the free-floating rationale becomes a reflected rationale, that is, a "reason." By acting deliberately, that is, after conscious consideration of the reason for the action, humans have developed a very powerful strategy for thriving in their environment. While language is itself developed by evolution, once developed, it acts as a crane—an accelerator for further evolution.

To help us understand the importance of linguistic reasons, Dennett offers us a framework for the various design options available to nature for the brain: the Tower of Generate-and-Test. On the ground level of the tower are *Darwinian creatures*, those that generate genetic mutations which produce hardwired phenotypes that are tested by the environment and either survive or become extinct.

Eventually some organisms develop that are only partially hard-wired and permit some level of phenotypic plasticity, namely, the ability to learn—the second story of the Tower. These *Skinnerian creatures* are designed to generate a variety of actions, discover which actions are effective in their environment, extinguish the ineffective ones, and rely on the surviving actions for the rest of the life of the individual.

On the third story of the Tower we have a further refinement: *Popperian creatures* are able to evaluate possible actions even before trying them for the first time. They generate hypotheses in some sort of inner environment and test them there before trying them in the external environment. As humans, we are Popperian creatures who are smart enough to permit our hypotheses to die in our stead. We are not alone; many animals are able to use information from their environments to select their best options before actually acting. Popperian creatures are designed by evolution to be intelligent, to preselect their behaviors on the basis of information from their natural environment.

On the next level of the Tower are *Gregorian creatures* who go beyond Popperian strategies because they take account of the designed portions of the outer environment. Once we become capable of recognizing tools—objects designed for a purpose—our intelligence for dealing with the world is greatly enhanced. Tools embody information about how best to act. To recognize an axe is to know how to chop down a tree. The most important tools are mind-tools, such as language, for they allow us to generate and test our options in the social world, in the environment in which there are other language-using minds like our own. Gregorian creatures are especially adept at social intelligence.

The top level of the Tower is science: the deliberate, foresightful Generate-and-Test procedures that, by relying on the activities of others in the community, allow us to cumulatively design our strategies for dealing with the world. Science is a superior mind-tool that has joined all our brains together into one cognitive system. This makes humans unique and puts us right off the scale of animal intelligence.

The Tower of Generate-and-Test brings out Dennett's claim that reasons, like meanings, evolve gradually. Beginning with a world governed entirely by physical, causal laws, evolution designs biological organisms, that is, entities with free-floating rationales.

Through various, gradual stages, these rationales eventually become represented by the organism, that is, they become reflective "reasons." As "rational animals" humans are indeed unique, but this special status does not imply that we are in some way beyond nature, that we transcend the natural world. Like meanings, reasons have evolved within nature through intermediate stages that were not yet reasons in the full sense. Instead of the essentialist approach that human nature is the incarnation of an eternal essence, Dennett shows how we can understand our humanity as the product of an adaptationist history.

The human mind is distinctive in that it goes beyond biological adaptation: it is the product of culture. Culture can be thought of as a set of brain programs that are transmitted, not by genes, but by learning passed on from generation to generation. This technique is much more rapid than the transmission of genetically based programs and so qualifies as a crane, for it speeds up the evolutionary process enormously.

Culture, as Dennett analyzes it, transmits discrete units of programming information that, following Dawkins, he calls memes. While the term "meme" is derived from "memetic" and refers to imitation, it resonates with "gene" and indeed memes play a role in cultural evolution analogous to the role of genes in genetic evolution. A meme is any unit of cultural or imitative transmission.

Examples of memes include use of the wheel, wearing clothes, writing with alphabets, playing chess, relying on calendars, singing Greensleeves, thinking in terms of Darwinian evolution. The tune Greensleeves, for instance, has survived and replicated for centuries because it is catchy, easy to remember, simple to play, has high prestige, and similar factors. Other tunes from the 16th century lacked some of these survival qualities and so are no longer around.

The relationship of memes to genes is not simply analogy. Since Dennett understands evolution as algorithmic, as a procedure that is medium neutral, memetic evolution is just as valid a realization of Darwin's Idea as is biological evolution. Within the medium of culture, memes are inherited in a stable fashion from generation to generation, they undergo mutation from time to time, and the resources that they need—e.g., mental space—are in limited supply; therefore memes must compete for survival. These are exactly the conditions required for the evolutionary algorithm.

As units of information, memes have a certain independence from their vehicle. Greensleeves may repeat like an earworm in someone's head, it may be transmitted as the printed score in a book of music, or it may be preserved in digital form on a CD. As information, the meme's material realization is secondary. This may seem like a disanalogy with genes, which have always been realized in biochemical form, but in fact it is not. That genes have always been encoded in DNA is an incidental feature of their function: if some day we were to create prosthetic DNA out of silicon chips, the gene, the genetic function, would not change. Like memes, genes are units of information, a point that brings out clearly the medium-neutral nature of Darwin's algorithm: it applies equally to both.

Characterizing memes as units of information may leave the mistaken impression that they are always passive. Memes, like genes, are more like programs than data: they restructure the brain so that it operates differently. A guitarist who has learned Greensleeves has a new ability; she has been reprogrammed so she can perform new actions. Memes can therefore be cumulative: the meme for making fire prepares the brain to receive memes for cooking, smelting, or making smoke signals. The meme for divine commandments programs the brain so that it is prepared to accept specific prohibitions. Above all, a brain programmed for language is greatly enriched in its ability to take on other, linguistically transmitted, memes. Culture is a crane capable of producing further cranes.

Memes that survive are the "fit" ones: those that have the appropriate features to replicate in their environment. They are, in this sense, "selfish memes." Since they are carried by human cultures and brains, memes that totally destroy these carriers could not survive in the long term; but this does not imply that every meme that replicates successfully contributes to the fitness of its hosts. Bravery in war is a meme that replicates well despite reducing the host's—the soldier's—chances of survival. Celibacy replicates well in certain religious environments, though its individual hosts do not reproduce. In cultural environments, "survival of the fittest" refers to the fitness and survival of the meme itself, not of its host.

Dennett is now in a position to define the human mind: the mind is "itself an artifact created when memes restructure a human brain to make it a better habitat for memes" (DDI 365). Reasons and meanings can now be transmitted memetically from brain to brain. Humans have not only evolved genetically, but have also been programmed by culture and language to be able to receive and propagate new ideas and so continue the process of evolution on the memetic level.

REDUCTIONISM

Does this account preserve human dignity? In the 19th century, opponents of Darwin's evolutionary theory believed that integrating human nature into biological evolution would reduce human dignity to the status of the apes. Does Dennett escape this reductionist charge?

"Reductionism" has many meanings and is sometimes used, without content, as a question-begging insult. If we give the term the rather bland meaning of coherently unifying human existence with the physical, chemical, and biological natural world order, then Dennett's approach is reductionist. Yet this kind of reductionism is innocuous to human dignity. There are still human beings with minds who operate on the level of reason and meaning, who learn new ideas from others and use these ideas to guide their lives. All that is excluded is the appeal to supernatural or spiritual skyhooks, an appeal that is incapable of explaining minds, reasons, and meanings in any case.

Another meaning of reductionism is the claim that there is nothing to human nature but the physical or the biological and so human dignity is an illusion. Dennett labels this position "greedy reductionism," and rejects it. Dennett's approach does not reduce the cultural to the biological, for the principle of adaptation turns out not to be a biological one. By interpreting Darwin's dangerous idea as a medium-neutral algorithm, Dennett offers a theory that integrates biological and cultural phenomena under one unifying principle that is neither specifically biological nor specifically cultural. His is an over-arching theory that explains genes and memes as but particular cases of the survival-of-the-fittest algorithm—an algorithm that may also explain other phenomena, e.g., computer viruses. Far from being a greedy reductionist, Dennett synthesizes previously disparate phenomena under the umbrella of a new scientific vision: "In a single stroke, the idea of evolution by natural selection unifies the realm of life, meaning and purpose with the realm of space and time, cause and effect, mechanism and physical law" (DDI 21).

We are now ready, in Chapter 5, to see how a human mind can develop into a person, a responsible self.

SELFHOOD: MEMES, LANGUAGE, AND NARRATIVE

Each of us is a self. I am the one who sees the world, who thinks about it, who makes decisions, and who directs my body in its actions. But what exactly is a "self"? Some think of the self as like the driver of a car, an entity that is different from the mechanism of the car but which controls that mechanism. For Descartes, the self is a different thing than the body, a *res cogitans* rather than a *res extensa*, a nonmaterial entity lodged in a material body. While Descartes himself explicitly rejects the analogy with a pilot in a ship, "Cartesianism" nevertheless promotes the image of the self as a separate, nonmaterial substance, a "soul-pearl."

David Hume, in the 18th century, famously challenged this conception. When he looks inward, he claimed, he finds impressions, ideas, thoughts, and so on, but no self, no I, no ego. Rephrasing Hume's search, Dennett tracks the passage of information inward from senses—the afferent processes—through the neurons of the brain to the motor cortex and then back out to the muscles on the periphery—the efferent processes—and claims that at no point along this loop do we find a neuron-self, or even a brain area that can be identified as a thing called a self.

So is the self an illusion? Obviously not! It is obvious that I am the one writing this text; it is obvious that you are reading it. Yet it is equally obvious to the neurophysiologist—as it was to Hume— that neither examination of the brain nor introspection by the mind reveals an entity called the self. "When a simple question gets two answers, 'Obviously yes!' and 'Obviously no!', a middle-ground position is worth considering, even though it is bound to be initially counterintuitive to all parties . . . ," says Dennett (CE 413).

Dennett's own position is that there is indeed a self, but that the concept must be demythologized. The self, as we normally understand and experience it, cannot be taken at face value. On the one hand, we need to uncover the underlying mechanism that produces and sustains it; on the other, we must reveal the gradual development that is concealed by the all-or-nothing conception common sense gives us. Dennett as usual steers the middle course: between the conception of the self as a thing or substance and the total rejection of the self as an illusion, he offers us a concept of the self as a mode of organization that is neither a thing nor an illusion. To grasp this concept, we must look at the evolution of selfhood, at the distinctively human notion of a responsible agent, and, above all, examine the role of language in its construction as a narrative structure. We will look at each of these in turn.

EARLY SELVES

In evolution, selfhood develops gradually from structures that are not selves in the human sense. Just as early sexual reproduction seems singularly unsexy from the human point of view, so the origins of selfhood do not look "selfy" to us. Take the case of a lobster: it differentiates its own limbs, which it does not eat, from other organisms in the environment that it uses as food. This is a kind of minimal self-recognition. Similarly, an automaton could be programmed to treat its own parts differently than objects in its environment. Even in humans, the same phenomenon can be found in our immune systems, which can identify interlopers to be attacked as different from cells that belong to our own bodies: the self-nonself distinction used by physiologists.

This kind of minimal "selfhood" is an essential feature of any organism. To remain a unity, any organism must have boundaries that distinguish that part of the world which it unifies and preserves from the rest of the world whose integrity is of no interest to it. Such self-boundaries are not purely spatial and need not coincide with the skin of an organism. The virus my immune system attacks as nonself is spatially inside my skin. A hermit crab adopts an empty shell from a different species and incorporates it within its own selfhood, although it is spatially outside its skin. Even a beaver's dam or a spider's web can be considered an extended phenotype insofar as it functions as part of the apparatus that preserves the integrity of the beaver or spider.

A self is not an object, but a mode of organization. To say of an organism that it has a self (in this minimal sense) is to say that it is structured so that processes in the organism differentiate between what "belongs" to the organism and what is foreign. Nor is a minimal self a representation: the hermit crab does not represent itself as having a shell. The crab does not know—in any reflective way—that the shell is part of its self. It doesn't know it has a self at all. Nor does a spider decide to create an "extended phenotype." There is no question of a spider making a conscious decision to spin a web. It just does it. It is programmed to do it automatically, as part of its nature.

While a human, selfy self is very different in many ways from such a minimal self, it shares some of these features. A human self, claims Dennett, is a mode of organization, not an object; it is part of our extended phenotype; and it comes about automatically: every normal human being unconsciously (initially) spins a web of selfhood.

HUMAN SELVES

Unlike a spider, the self that a human spins is a web of narrative rather than of silk. Such narratives can still be seen as extensions of the organism, extensions that allow it to integrate its dealings with the world over both space and time. We can distinguish two stages in this extension: it is founded on representations of the body; then it develops by constructing responsible agency.

First, the brain must monitor the body; the brain needs to know which thing in the world the body is. Dennett uses the analogy of a shared radar system for small boats. A land-based radar transmits a television image to all boats in its area. As a boat owner I can then see blips that represent the boats nearby. But which one am I? I change course and watch to see which blip moves accordingly. Similarly for the body: if I tangle my arms and fingers with other people's so that I become confused about whose hand I am seeing, I have only to move my own finger to be able to spot which visual element represents my own hand. By these and similar techniques I keep track of—that is, represent—those parts of the world that make up my own body. Dennett describes this as the "basic blip" of self-representation.

The basic blip is just the basis, for the self is not only a physical or spatial organization. The self is an agent; it is the source of action. While my feet walk along the trail, my eyes perceive the trees, and my fingers scratch an insect bite. These spatially disparate activities are all integrated into one coherent unity: they are all mine. They are the actions of one agent. In a similar way, as a self, I am an organized unity over time. We might sometimes think of conscious processes, or of actions and social relationships, as existing for an isolated moment in time, but such an idea is at best an abstraction invented for the purpose of some particular intellectual analysis. An isolated mental act, an individual conscious state can do little on its own. Perhaps the idea is useful as a foil to bring out by contrast the essentially temporal nature of the self. In reality, I am not a momentary, extensionless point: I am smeared over time. The commitments I made yesterday determine the obligations I have today; the vows I make today are the reason that I will wake up married tomorrow. Looked at as isolated instants in time, none of these attributes of the self would make any sense. They could not be the actions of an agent. As an agent, I do not exist at a point; as Dennett puts it, we must abandon the notion of a "punctuate self" (FE 122n).

An agent is responsible for its actions. Responsibility can only be attributed to a being that, while extended in space and time, is integrated in an organized and appropriate manner. As an agent, I must track not only which body is mine, and which actions are under my control, I must also know what kinds of actions they are: Am I fighting or fleeing? Am I lying or telling the truth? I must therefore monitor not just the situation of my body in space, but also the internal or "mental" situation: the reasons and motives that allow me to identify and understand the action I am performing. This is the reflective component of human selfhood without which responsible agency would be impossible.

The self, in so far as it is a mode of organizing, has flexible boundaries. I can make my self small or large. I can define a knee-jerk reflex or an immune reaction as an event that happens to me rather than an action that my self is responsible for. Under other circumstances a car I am driving can be incorporated into my self so that I sense the traction of the tires on the road, experience a left turn as my action, and feel the potential power I have for passing. I can treat my family or a sports team as part of my extended self and feel pride or shame for those actions that the group is responsible for. In Multiple Personality Disorder, a self may take responsibility for only a subset of the actions of its body, attributing the other actions to an alter, an other self. On the other extreme, there may be cases—some twins perhaps—where two bodies may each share only a part of one unified self. The boundaries of the self can expand or contract.

These cases, even the more speculative ones, bring out Dennett's point: a self is not an object or thing; it is a mode of organization. The eyes, directed at the trail, send neural information to the optical lobes that, after analysis, tell the brain I am on a trail; as a result, impulses from the frontal lobes cause the motor cortex to guide my walking feet between the trees. It is somewhere along this loop from input to output that Hume, and many others, have searched in vain for some *thing*, some object, called the self. The self, says Dennett, is not one stopping point or instant along the loop; it is the loop itself. The self is how these structures are organized.

> Once you distribute the work . . . in both time and space in the brain, you have to distribute the moral agency around as well. You are not out of the loop; you *are* the loop. You are that large. You are not an extensionless point. (FE 242)

The self, then, is that mode of organization that integrates—over both time and space—perception, action, and the mental springs of action. That's what it is to be one responsible agent.

This integrating organization depends on language. It is by language that we build up a defining story about ourselves, a story organized around the basic blip of self-representation that originates in physical and internal self-monitoring. It is language that gives rise to the "narrative self."

NARRATIVE SELFHOOD

Language initially evolves as a mode of communication with others but its arrival heralds an enormous transformation in the nature of brains. Once we start talking to others about our actions, we need to be able to keep track of what these actions are and why we are doing them. To explain to others what we are about, we need to be able to categorize our behavior and give motives or reasons for it.

Since the causes of our actions are very complex and involve competition between many parallel processes in the brain, any explanation we offer in language can capture only a snapshot of them: it is inevitably a simplification.

Language is not used just for communication with others: it leads to reflection—to communication with ourselves, as it were. Reflection requires language. Language may initially be needed in order to tell others the reasons for our actions, but once it exists, it supplies the concepts that allow us to become aware of our own mental processes. A dog may bark in anger but cannot reflect on the fact that it is angry. Once humans learn the term "anger" in the process of explaining their behavior to others, they may ask themselves the reason for an incipient behavior and use the concept to reflect on their own internal state—even if such reflection actually results in inhibiting the behavior itself. Self-consciousness, the consciousness of oneself, appears as a secondary result of our linguistic interaction with others.

Language not only results in self-awareness. It also enables us to issue commands—not just to others but to ourselves. We can set ourselves tasks—going to class, for instance—that would be impossible without the linguistic concepts involved. Language enables us to become chameleonic transformers: when we use language to take on new projects and adopt new rules and policies, we transform our mind from one virtual machine into another. Such self-commands allow the linguistic level of mind to control other processes, and this is the basis for voluntary action. An action is free in so far as it is the result of something I have asked myself to do. (More on freedom in Chapter 7.)

For Dennett, language does even more than enable communication, self-awareness, and voluntary action. Language generates stories or narratives, and these in turn create the self. Inverting common sense, Dennett holds that it is not the self that tells tales; initially at least, it is the narrative that generates the self. The distinctively human self is a narrative self and is a construct of language: "Our tales are spun, but for the most part we don't spin them; they spin us. Our human consciousness, and our narrative selfhood, is their product, not their source" (CE 418).

The idea that language precedes consciousness—"pandemonium"—is one we have already met in Chapter 3, but we must now flesh out the implications for the nature of the self.

A science-fiction scenario may help us. Imagine a computer that has been programmed to write novels. (Artificial intelligence programs have created poetry and music, so a novel is not too much of a stretch.) Suppose that one story our computer produces appears to be an autobiography: "Call me Gilbert . . .," it starts. We have stipulated that the computer is just a machine: it is not conscious and cannot think. And Gilbert is, of course, fictional. Nevertheless, we can interpret the text as a series of adventures that center on Gilbert, our fictional character. Let us elaborate this thought-experiment by embedding this computer in a robot with videocams, a speaker system and perhaps wheels. Careful programming allows the ongoing autobiography to be modified by the real circumstances and events in the world around the robot. If you knock it with a baseball bat, for instance, the subsequent section of the story will involve an individual, whose description matches you, hitting Gilbert with a bat. It now appears as if the text, as we interpret it, is a heterophenomenological report, the report of someone's experience. But whose?

In our earlier reference to the novels of Conan Doyle, in Chapter 3, we distinguished Sherlock Holmes, as a character in the content of the novels, from the author and the process of writing. In our current scenario, there is no author: the novel-writing computer/robot is simply a machine. Hence there is even less temptation to say that the writer is the subject of the experience recounted. It is to "Gilbert" that we must attribute the experience. Gilbert is neither the name of the machine nor the name of the program that generates the novel. Gilbert is the protagonist within the heterophenomenological report created by the computer. Within the text, Gilbert might claim to be the author of the report, but we, of course, know that he is mistaken. He is a character within the novel produced by the computer program. It is not just conscious experience that is generated by the mechanisms of language generation in the brain: the very existence of the self has the same status. Like Gilbert, every self is a construct created by an impersonal—that is, unselflike—process of language production in the brain.

Whatever we might think of the analogy with novel-writing computers, Dennett's position is that the self is a construct of evolutionary, linguistic, social, and neural factors. He refers to it as an *abstractum*, as an abstract object. "It is, if you like, a theorist's fiction. It is not one of the real things in the universe in addition to the atoms" (CNG). He frequently compares its abstract theoretical status with that of a center of gravity. In physics, any object with mass has a center of gravity, a mathematical point that allows us to calculate the behavior of the object as a whole. A center of gravity is not a piece or component of the object; in the case of the table, for example, the center of gravity is often a point in midair between the legs, outside any of the matter that the table is composed of. Yet this does not mean that a center of gravity is an illusion. It is an extremely useful concept: a physicist who denied its existence or considered it invalid would be foolish indeed, for she would undermine her ability to explain and predict the physical world. Nevertheless, unlike a thing such as a table, it is an abstract entity defined within a theory.

> A self, according to my theory, is not any old mathematical point, but an abstraction defined by the myriads of attributions and interpretations (including self-attributions and self-interpretations) that have composed the biography of the living body whose Center of Gravity it is. (CE 426–427)

Like a center of gravity, the self is, as we have seen, a simplification. At any moment there are many processes going on in the brain: some competing for control over motor reactions; some winning; some losing. Language, in contrast, is linear: we can only say one thing at a time. When we interact with other people, what we say necessarily simplifies the myriad of parallel processes. We must be able to give one coherent reason for our action. Just as a center of gravity allows us to ignore the inertial properties of the individual parts of each table leg, so operating with the concept of a self allows us to get beyond the detailed functioning of multiple brain processes and deal with the person as a whole. It is on the level of this simplified whole that the self exists. Dennett compares it to the user interface of a computer, which also vastly simplifies the complex internal processes. Without a simplified global structure that action can be attributed to, we would be unable to present ourselves to others as unified entities. The same simplification is involved when we represent ourselves to ourselves: the linear stream of consciousness, as we saw in Chapter 3, is an artefact that rides on the buzzing confusion of underlying processes.

From this point of view, it is a mistake, in looking for the self, to search for a Boss neuron, or for some other kinglike entity in the brain. The self is more like an ambassador or press secretary, a public relations agent who speaks for the person as a whole. When a press release is attributed to a "spokesperson for the prime minister's office," the speaker is not expressing their own opinion: they are issuing a statement that may well be the compromise result of struggles between various coalitions of advisers, a result that no single individual may actually agree with. Indeed, the release may have been written by a committee, so the "spokesperson" may be a complete abstraction. As the various advisers form different and fluctuating coalitions, the coalition whose opinion is being expressed may vary from time to time depending on the power dynamics, even though the various statements are all attributed to the same "spokesperson for the PMO." The self is a kind of figurehead like this, a Head of Mind, the author of record, to whom speech acts are attributed, even though the language module may be influenced by different coalitions of mental processes from time to time.

The self, therefore, like any mode of organization, must be attributed globally. Say I am explaining a word processor program to a novice. I explain how the keyboard operates, how letters are represented, how line-wrapping works, how the results are displayed on the screen or the printer, and so on. At the end, the novice says, "I understand each of these processes, but you forgot to tell me which of them is the word processor." Clearly she has missed the whole point. "Word processor" is the name of all the components taken together: it would be a category mistake to attribute the term to any subcomponent. Similarly, "self" is a term that is applied globally to the organized totality of perception, action, narrative, responsibility, and social interrelationships.

In so far as the self is a mode of organization that depends on narrative, it has a certain independence from the body. Just as a computer program, which is a particular mode of organization of information, can be taken off one computer and run on another, if the narrative process that creates and sustains my selfhood could be moved to a different body than my own, or even perhaps to a silicon chip-based system, then theoretically I, the same self as before, would survive. If our longing is for immortality, for surviving the death of the body, we would do better to place our hope in the persistence of the narrative process rather than in the everlasting life of a soul-pearl.

STATUS OF THE SELF

Dennett's claim that the self is not a soul-pearl but a construct is frequently interpreted to mean that it is an illusion. I think this is a misinterpretation. It is true that he frequently speaks of the self as a fiction, as a theorist's fiction, just as centers of gravity are fictions. But the word "fiction" is ambiguous: it is used in at least two ways. On the one hand it can have a negative connotation when it is used to refer to something as false, as invalid or unreal: "The defendant's account of events was pure fiction." On the other hand it can be used to emphasize the constructed or created aspect of a literary work, a very positive notion. I think it is this second, constructed aspect of selfhood that Dennett is trying to bring out. What he is rejecting is the conceptualization of the self as a thing, as a soul. He says:

> The task of constructing a self that can *take* responsibility is a major social and educational project, and you are right to be concerned about threats to its integrity. But a brain-pearl, a real, "intrinsically responsible" whatever-it-is, is a pathetic bauble to brandish like a lucky charm in the face of this threat. The only hope, and not at all a forlorn one, is to come to understand, naturalistically, the ways in which brains grow self-representations, thereby equipping the bodies they control with responsible selves. (CE 429–430)

It is only as an entity constructed in this way that the self can act on the basis of reflected reasons and so take responsibility for its actions. The self exists as the result of the evolution of social interactions that require each human animal to create within itself a mode of organization for interacting with others, a subsystem that, once created, allows it to interact with itself at different times. Narrative is the mode of this organization. In speaking of myself— and others speaking of me—as the agent of record, relationships are established between past, present, and future perceptions and actions, and it is the global attribution of these to the center of narrative gravity that is the self. Only by understanding the self in this way is it possible for Dennett to offer a coherent account of free will, of the rational freedom that selfhood makes possible—free will is the topic of Chapter 7. Dennett's bottom line is that moral action is real and valid. As he puts it, "[We develop a] perspective on ourselves, a place from which to *take* responsibility. The name for this Archimedean perch is the self" (FE 259). Is such a constructed self not "real" enough?

The answer may depend on what we mean by "real." It is time we bit the bullet and faced the fundamental question that has been lurking for too long: What is Dennett's ontology? What is "reality?"

CHAPTER 6

ONTOLOGY: STANCES, PATTERNS, AND REALISM

The discussion about the reality of selves leads us to a more fundamental question: what it is to be "real"? The investigation of the nature of reality is called ontology—from the Greek term *ons*, a being. In the Western tradition, ontologists are often divided into realists and idealists. Realists hold that the world is made up of beings that are "in-themselves," that is, whose nature and existence are independent of knowing or perceiving subjects. Descartes can be counted as a realist because he holds that there are substances, physical, spiritual, and divine, that have within themselves the power to exist whether anyone knows them or not. Berkeley, on the other hand, is the paradigm of an idealist: he holds that all things are actually ideas in the mind. Dennett, in characteristic fashion, rejects both of these traditional camps and adopts an alternative ontological position. He calls the position "mild realism," though choosing this label, he muses, is probably a tactical mistake.

To understand mild realism we will first look at Dennett's theory that objects depend on physical, design, and intentional stances, and then discuss the idea of stances as such. Underlying the somewhat idealist notion of stances are real patterns, which reestablish Dennett's claim to be a realist. Examining the attribution of belief will bring the debate about the realist or idealist status of mental states into focus. The chapter finishes by explaining the relevance of the stance approach to the issues of consciousness, evolution, and selfhood that we have already examined.

STANCES

Imagine my task is to predict the behavior of a pocket calculator. What will happen if I press in succession the three keys 2 + 2? An obvious strategy is to assume that, since it has been designed to perform arithmetic calculations, the calculator's display will show a 4. At least, that is what it *should* show, if it is working properly. Of course I could adopt an alternative predictive strategy: I could dismantle the calculator and track the passage of electrons in accordance with physical laws through the myriad of circuits they follow from the key presses to the atoms in the LCD display. While this alternative, physical strategy is always possible in principle, it would be a very time-consuming task, and, if presented with a new model of calculator, the task would have to be repeated anew all over again. The first strategy, which assumes that the calculator will do what it is designed to do, is faster, more practical, and works on any model. Its predictions, however, are not perfect: on rare occasions, when the calculator malfunctions and does not do what it is "supposed" to do, the design strategy will get it wrong and only the more elaborate prediction based on physical laws will be accurate. Dennett labels the first predictive strategy the design stance and the second, based on the laws of physics, the physical stance.

In some cases, a third predictive strategy works. When playing chess, I may predict that if I move my bishop to a certain square, my opponent, believing that I am threatening her queen, and wanting to preserve the valuable piece, will take my bishop. My predictive strategy involves attributing a belief to her—that I am threatening her queen—and a desire—that she wants to preserve her queen—and assuming that, as a rational agent, she will act on the basis of this belief and this desire. Dennett refers to this third strategy as the intentional stance. An alien, who knew nothing of chess players, might dismantle my opponent, figure out what each part of her brain was designed to do, and so predict her move from the design stance. This would be a massive task that he is unlikely to be able to complete before the clock rings for the next move. An even less practical strategy would be to ignore the functions her brain circuits were designed for and track the physical operations that underpin them. Given the heuristic time constraints, the intentional strategy is a much more practical approach that gives the right prediction most, though not all, of the time.

The strategic nature of stances means that the question of which one should be used cannot always be given a definitive answer. We could attribute to a thermostat the "belief" that the room is too cold and the "desire" to warm it up, but the strategy would give us no predictive advantage over the design stance. It would be not so much wrong as pointless in practice. On the other hand, meeting a polar bear on the ice in early spring, it would be very impractical of an Inuit hunter to adopt the physical or designed stance—though the results would not be false; attributing to the bear the desire to eat and the belief that the hunter is edible is the only predictive strategy likely to allow evasive action within the time constraints. When a newborn baby latches onto a nipple, should we say the action is due to genetic design or should we attribute the belief that the nipple will supply milk? How about a one-year-old? Dennett thinks that in many cases like these there is no definitively best strategy. In attributing belief, we are not dealing with any "fact of the matter," but rather with the practical issue of which stance is the more or less successful under the circumstances.

When the intentional stance turns out in practice to be the most successful in predicting the behavior of an entity, we define the entity as an intentional system. This definition ignores the internal structure of the entity. A chess opponent is an intentional system if the intentional stance predicts its behavior. The opponent may be a human being or a computer, but this fact is irrelevant to defining its status as an intentional system. In a similar way, that a thermostat is labelled a design system depends on the success of the design stance and not on the internal physical structure of the device; whether it is made up of electronic, mechanical, or biological components is irrelevant to the labelling.

In abstracting in this way from the underlying mechanism, each stance establishes a certain normativity. The design stance can predict the behavior of a thermostat only if the thermostat behaves as it *should*. The stance sets up a norm, and if the thermostat violates that norm, it is declared to be broken, to have malfunctioned, and so the design stance will no longer be a successful predictive strategy. Similarly, the intentional stance sets up expectations about what an intentional system *should* believe, or should desire. If I predict that an oncoming pedestrian will keep to her side and pass me, but instead she turns and walks into me—maybe she is epileptic—then

I declare her "irrational," that is, someone for whom the intentional stance is no longer predictive.

If the pedestrian does keep to her side, I understand her action. While Dennett first introduces stances as strategies of prediction, they are also modes of understanding. Each of these three stances allows us a particular way of understanding the world. When we grasp the design of a thermostat, we thereby understand it and its behavior. We see someone running and are curious why. The explanation that the person wants to win a race and believes that training in advance will allow them to do so resolves this curiosity (though it may now make us curious about why she wants to win a race).

Each of Dennett's stances brings with it a mode of understanding, a set of categories or concepts, a set of appropriate questions, and an ensemble of paradigms for explanation that are proper to it. The *function* of any process, for instance, is a notion that makes sense from the design stance. It is not just that function or purpose cannot be discovered from the physical stance; the concept makes no sense, it does not even arise, in the physical approach. Similarly, *belief* and *desire* are completely invisible from the design stance. Each stance has its own world: a set of objects and categories revealed by it that other stances are blind to.

As modes of understanding, the stances are interrelated. The runner's training only makes sense because it exercises her heart whose function is to pump blood—the design stance—and such pumping can itself be explained on physical principles. Nevertheless, the stances have a certain independence from each other. Even if we understand the design of the human body perfectly and so can predict that exercise would increase the capacity of the heart, if we fail to grasp the runner's motive, there is something fundamental about the situation that we do not understand. Similarly, someone who came across a thermostat could examine the mechanism and be able to explain the physical principles for each of its operations yet fail to grasp that the function of a thermostat is to maintain a steady temperature. The design stance permits a level of understanding that the physical stance cannot provide.

REALITY OF BELIEFS

Stances permit prediction and understanding in part by categorizing the situation in terms of certain objects. What is the status of these objects that are revealed only from a stance? Is the pumping function of the heart objective and real? Are there really beliefs? This raises the basic ontological question: the issue of realism. What is it for something to be "real"? Dennett focuses primarily on the reality of beliefs, though his discussion can be generalized to objects in any stance.

The intentional stance attributes beliefs (as well as desires, reasons, etc.) to intentional systems. If part of the explanation for my behavior of feeding fish to my cat is the belief that "cats eat fish," is there really such a belief in my head? Are beliefs real or are they just explanatory fictions?

One approach to the question is instrumentalism: beliefs are not real but simply part of the apparatus used for explanation, one of the conceptual instruments used for predicting the world but not part of the world itself. When a physicist, for instance, uses the traditional parallelogram to analyse the components of forces, he is not suggesting that this represents anything real in the world—it is simply a calculating technique. While, as we will see, there are various kinds of instrumentalists, traditional, full-blown instrumentalists held that almost all scientific concepts were instruments in this sense: parallelograms, forces, gravity, atoms, electrons, and so on did not represent realities in the world; they were simply components of our calculative schemes. An instrumentalist would maintain that attributing beliefs to thermostats, chess computers, animals, or humans might be a useful way of predicting behavior, but that such beliefs are pure fictions, ways we interpret the world. They are temporary pragmatic expedients, part of our interpretative scheme, and do not exist in reality. The position verges on idealism—at least for scientific objects.

On the opposite extreme are realists. They say that anyone who claims that I believe cats eat fish is committed to the existence of some entity or structure in my head—physical, functional, cognitive, or spiritual—that is the real belief, the fact of the matter, that warrants the claim. The belief is a real, in-itself, object that exists whether or not anyone knows it, and whether or not anyone adopts the intentional stance. It is a belief because of its own intrinsic nature. Dennett calls such people strong or "industrial strength" realists.

There are a number of difficulties with strong realism about beliefs. First, there is the almost infinity of linguistic descriptions or specifications for each belief. If I believe that cats eat fish, then I must also believe that cats eat (some) vertebrates, that cats eat animals, that cats eat objects, and so on. I must also believe that cats eat at least one of cod, salmon, mackerel, etc. For almost any propositional beliefs offered, we can spin off a myriad of other beliefs that can be correctly attributed to me. A realist seems to have to maintain that each of these already exists as a real entity in my head. This seems implausible: my head is too small! Then there is a difficulty with "undecidables." Someone with dementia puts their alarm clock in the freezer. Do they believe the freezer is a cabinet? Do they believe that the alarm clock is a fish? That it is food? A realist appears to be committed to there being a fact of the matter: there is some definite belief in their head, even if we do not know what it is. Does a dog, having no language, still believe that what it has buried is a bone, a chicken bone, a femur, or part of the anatomy of some animal? The realist position seems to require that beliefs be identified, specified, and individuated in some intrinsic manner once and for all.

Predictably, Dennett rejects both extremes, both pure instrumentalism and interpretationism, on the one hand, and strong realism, on the other. Mental states are neither instrumental fictions nor "in-themselves" real. He holds that the specification of beliefs depends on the context of attribution, on the role they play in explanation and prediction from the intentional stance.

> My thesis will be that while belief is a perfectly objective phenomenon (that apparently makes me a realist), it can be discerned only from the point of view of one who adopts a certain *predictive strategy*, and its existence can be confirmed only by an assessment of the success of that strategy (that apparently makes me an interpretationist). (IS 15)

What can we make of this position? How is it possible for a claim that can be made only from within a stance to be objective? Is it not essentially relative?

One can start by responding that such stance-relativism is not a relativism about truth or objectivity. It is not a claim that what is true for you might be false for me. Harvey's claim in the 17th century that the function of the heart is to pump blood is objectively true; Descartes' competing claim that the function of the heart is to heat blood is objectively false. Such objective truth or falsity, however, is only valid from the design stance. This is not relativism in the pernicious sense that what is true from the design stance might be false from the physical stance. The physical stance does not contradict or disagree with Harvey's position: the question of the function of the heart does not arise at all for the physical stance. Functions are not its concern: the category of function or purpose plays no role in physical explanation. Similarly, intentional stance claims about belief or desire do not enter into the design stance. The claim that truth is relative to a stance is therefore not relativism in the noxious sense that what is true from one point of view might be false from another. The theory of stances does not undermine objectivity. It is rather *a theory of* objectivity: objectivity is not simply in-itself, but depends on a stance. Functions are real. Beliefs are real. Nevertheless, neither are absolute realities that could exist independently of their appropriate stances. Though Dennett says less about them, physical realities, such as gravity or neutrinos, are presumably in the same boat: their reality is not absolute but makes sense only within the physical stance. There are different kinds of reality.

For strong realists, who believe there is only one kind of reality, truth seems to be a simple matter of correspondence: a proposition is true if it corresponds to how things are in themselves. Propositions predicate properties of objects: the box weighs 6 g; the heart's function is to pump blood; John has the belief that cats eat fish. When such sentences are objectively true, they correspond to how things are, to the facts of the matter.

For Dennett, truth is more complicated. Each stance establishes a set of concepts, methods, strategies, and norms for success—a web of significance—and it is only from this perspective that objects and their predicates make sense. There are no substances that possess properties in isolation from their context, without reference to perspectives and strategies. Hence there can be no proposition that is true simply by corresponding to an independent, isolated fact. Dennett appears to have an alternative theory of predication based on attribution: a predicate can be attributed to an object only within a context, the context of a successful predictive strategy. "The function of the heart is to pump blood" is not a claim about how things are "in-themselves": it attributes this function only from the design stance. Within this stance, a function is not a simple fact: apart from being contextual, it is normative. If a heart does not pump blood, it has failed in its function; it is broken. Attributions are value-laden and tell us how things *should* be. In Dennett's words:

> I have held that since *any* attributions of function necessarily invoke optimality or rationality assumptions, the attributions of intentionality that depend on them are *interpretations* of the phenomena—a "heuristic overlay" . . ., describing an inescapably idealized "real pattern". (BC 360)

Within each stance there are ways of determining whether attribution is successful, in which case the statement is true. Yet its truth is contextual, not absolute.

Attribution is, because of its contextual nature, holistic. Attributing the belief that cats eat fish to John as one global entity allows us to predict what he will feed his cat for supper. This does not mean, however, that Dennett limits us to a black box perspective. Ryle, Wittgenstein, and some psychological behaviorists suggest that, while we can attribute mental properties to an organism as a whole, internal structures are logically closed to us. As we've already seen, Dennett is emphatically not a "behaviourist," a term that he "abhors"—at least when it is applied to him. Dennett's holism is different: while the intentional stance is the global precondition for any attribution of belief, the contribution of internal processes to the belief is open to empirical investigation. We could in principle discover (indeed Dennett believes it is quite likely we will) that identifying some internal processes of an organism as the place where a certain belief resides may be a good strategy for prediction. What is important for his position is that the belief status of such processes is derivative from the global intentional stance; it reflects the role the process plays in the success of the predictive strategy.

This is why it is pointless to attribute beliefs to a thermostat. Within a thermostat, treating a switch position as a belief gives us no increase in predictive power over viewing it from the design stance. We could imagine circumstance in which it could become predictive. If the switch responded not only to low temperature, but to people shivering, to ice forming on the window, to plants wilting, and so on, then the roles that it would play in response to many different circumstances in the world would become more complex.

In the limit, the roles might become so complex that the intentional attribution, "it believes the room is cold," would in practice be the best way for us to predict its behavior. It is the complexity of its contextual relationships with the world, the richness of its embeddedness in its situation, that would move us toward attributing to the switch the predicate "believes that it is cold." This is a matter of multiple realization. That many different situations in the world all have for it the same meaning, "it is cold," is what moves us from the physical or design stance to the intentional. In the complex situation, the only property that the myriads of potential stimuli have in common is their significance for the entity. In this case it is only from the viewpoint of meaning, that is, from the intentional stance, that it is practical to make predictions. In the end, that a human being has beliefs and a thermostat does not is a matter of the complexity of our embeddedness in the world and the impracticality of dealing with this complexity from a physical or design stance. It is not that humans have souls while thermostats do not.

Does this make Dennett a reductionist? If there are no souls—in the sense of separate spiritual entities—and the only difference between human and thermostats is complexity, is he not reducing the world of beliefs, desires, and thoughts to the world of matter? Dennett rejects the charge.

The point about the three stances is that no stance has an ultimate privilege. While Dennett accepts the validity of the physical stance, he does not hold that the physical stance has exclusive or ultimate access to reality. He is a materialist, but he denies that he is a physicalist.

Yet neither is he a pure functionalist. We have seen (in Chapters 1 and 3) that Dennett is very sympathetic to functionalism and uses it as the jumping off point for his philosophy of mind. In the end, however, function is a design-level concept. Although the design stance has its legitimate place, beliefs cannot be attributed to brain processes on the basis of designed functions: belief is an intentional-level concept. It is true that, if belief attributions are predictive, there must be functions in the brain that make it possible for the organism to behave appropriately. The functions, however, do not define the belief, for it is possible that a different set of functions could implement the same belief. Once again, this is a matter of multiple realization. As an analogy, consider the fact that left- and right-handed people use somewhat different parts of the brain for language. This is a physical-level difference, but it may be the case that they process language differently too, that is, they use a different functional architecture for constructing sentences that, nevertheless, have the same meaning. The variation in the underlying process doesn't change the meaning. Analogously, it is the intentional context that makes a belief the one it is; different underlying functions do not influence its identity. It follows that intentional-level phenomena cannot be reduced to design-level ones.

Dennett's theory of stances is a rejection of greedy reductionism in general. While they may be tightly related, each stance has its own autonomy. Intentional concepts can no more be reduced to design concepts than design concepts can be reduced to the purely physical. There is no one kind of reality that trumps all others: the notion of "reality" is not a univocal concept, but a concept whose meaning varies with the stance adopted. While a greedy reductionist, an industrial strength realist, may have a single, simplistic notion of reality, Dennett, in opposition, holds that what makes something "real" is its role within a successful strategy of prediction. He is therefore not a hardcore reductionist.

But is he not, after all, an instrumentalist? Again, there is instrumentalism and instrumentalism. Initially, Dennett accepted to be called an instrumentalist, but later rejected the label when he discovered it was being misinterpreted. Those with a univocal concept of reality have a black-and-white dividing line between what is really real and what is purely illusory. For such people, traditional instrumentalist concepts fall on the illusory side: if they are not really real what else could they be but fictional? Since Dennett rejects this univocal approach to reality, he now holds that an instrumentalist interpretation of his position distorts it. There are different kinds of reality, each of them dependent on a stance. Being dependent on a stance does not make a concept illusory; on the contrary, it is only when a concept is understood as dependent upon a stance that it can be objectively real in any sense.

PATTERNS

The dependence of reality on stances might seem to align Dennett with various strands of antirealism and postmodernism. Some historians of science have suggested that all facts depend on theory. Structuralists claim that concepts, objects, and theories are generated by an underlying structure of knowledge. Postmodernists see objects as dependent on language, vocabulary, and concepts. Does Dennett's insistence that objectivity is stance-relative not ultimately align him with antirealists?

Dennett's answer is no. Committed as he is to the scientific worldview, he hankers after something solid, some ontological foundation that is as it is beyond the limitations of any stance. In an essay, "Real Patterns," which he describes as "utterly central to my thinking" (BC 95–120), he argues—against antirealists—that the predictive success of the stances "depends on there being some order or pattern in the world to exploit" (BC 98). The role of the stances is to capitalize on such real patterns, to recognize and conceptualize them, and to use them for prediction and control. No predictive strategy would be possible if patterns were not real.

So what is a pattern? Dennett starts with the notion of data, or information and the task of transmitting it. Sometimes we may transmit a complete string of data seriatim, as a bitmap, but this is often inefficient. A more efficient way is to compress the data—think of the reduced size of an MP3 compression of a wav file. Some sets of data are such that no compression is possible: the only way to transmit them is bit by bit, for any compression would necessarily lose some of the information. A series of data is said to be random if it is incompressible in principle. Dennett can now define a pattern as any data that are not random, i.e., data that are, to at least some extent, compressible without loss. "A pattern exists in some data—is real—if *there is* a description of the data that is more efficient than the bit map, whether or not anyone can concoct it" (BC 103).

In a set of data that has a pattern, some of the data may not be part of the pattern, that is, there may be "noise." Data is considered noise when it is not part of the particular pattern that we are interested in. It is quite possible that some or all of the noise may be part of a different pattern. In other words, there may be a number of different patterns in any dataset and so the distinction between patterned data and noise is relative to the pattern that concerns us. If different perceivers perceive different patterns, this may not be a disagreement: both perceivers may be "right," that is, both may have discerned a real pattern, though a different one. Choosing between such rival descriptions is a pragmatic matter: depending on our interests, one description or another may turn out to be empirically the better predictor of future events. Better does not necessarily mean more accurate: it is possible that the most accurate predictions may be the most costly in terms of time and resources. A fast, rough and ready prediction may well be a better bet than a more precise but, in practice, intractable calculation.

If we apply these principles to the evolutionary situation, where resources are scarce, we can see that adaptation is likely to favor rough and ready predictions over more accurate but time-consuming calculations. Sensing a possible predator, it was more important to take immediate evasive action than to achieve certainty about the identity of the stimulus. So we can see why organisms have come to rely on the design and intentional stances rather than the physical stance: while less accurate, they are faster. Remember the chess example: faced with an opponent in chess, predictions based on the physical stance might be in principle 100 percent correct, but they are intractable in practice. Predicting in terms of belief and desire—the opponent wants to take my queen!—even though less accurate, may allow me to win the game most of the time. Relying on the pattern revealed by the intentional stance is the better way—indeed the only practical way—to go.

Even within the intentional stance, there may be more than one pattern to discover in the noisy data. Did Jonah, the fisherman, believe that whales are fish? Maybe he just had a general conception of whales as animals that lived in the sea. Knowing little of biology, he may never have asked himself the relevant questions. Contemporary language, influenced by modern biology, may force any statement we make in English to pick out one precise pattern: a whale is a fish; or a whale is not a fish. The need to pin Jonah's state down in this way is an artefact of language; either statement may be more exact than Jonah's own thought. We should not allow this feature of language to foist onto us an overly precise ontology of beliefs or other mental states. A strong realist must say that in Jonah's head there is a fact of the matter, something that is really real, that makes one of these propositions true. Dennett disagrees: both attributions may pick out patterns that are predictively useful about Jonah, and so both beliefs are real—of course, "mildly" real.

> ... [T]here could be two different systems of belief attribution to an individual that differed *substantially* in what they attributed ... and yet no deeper fact of the matter could establish that one

was a description of the individual's *real* beliefs and the other not. That is, there could be two different, but equally real, patterns discernible in the noisy world. (BC 118)

SEMANTIC CAUSALITY

But, a strong realist might object, a causal analysis can resolve the ambiguity and deliver a fact of the matter. Is the ultimate test of reality not causal efficacy? Jonah's actions must ultimately be caused by one specific physical state, since it is what is physically real—the syntactical structure—in the brain that does the causal work. The semantic content of the syntactical structure may be open to more than one interpretation, but the semantic content itself cannot operate as a cause. A belief itself cannot be a cause; it is the physical structure that instantiates it in the brain that actually does the work. Causation is a concept on the physical level and cannot be legitimately used within the intentional stance. Hence there must be one "really" real structure that represents a belief after all. So goes the objection.

Dennett rejects this argument. He denies that causation is purely physical. As a predictive strategy, the intentional stance picks out patterns of real, empirical regularities that have every right to be considered causal. To support his argument, Dennett offers one of his most striking thought-experiments: the two semantic boxes.

Two boxes are discovered, A and B. One has three lamps: red, amber, and green. The other has two buttons: alpha and beta. They are joined by a cable. An investigation reveals, over millions of trials, that pressing button alpha on box A invariably results in the red lamp on box B lighting up, while pressing button beta turns on the green lamp. This is a very robust, empirically determined, causal regularity. Further investigation discovers that every button push generates a stream of 10,000 binary bits in the connecting cable—a different stream each time—and that these are fed into a supercomputer in box B that, after millions of operations, turns on either the red lamp or the green lamp. When investigators feed streams replicated from the output of box A into box B, they discover that the same stream will invariably produce the same result but, surprisingly, if the stream is modified, even by one bit, it is almost always the amber lamp that lights up. Opening box A, they find another supercomputer that takes input from button alpha—1—or button beta—0—and, after combining this input with a random number and calculating for some millions of operations, finally generates the 10,000 long stream of binary data fed out toward box B.

Tracing the microdetails of the processing of each bit through millions of cycles in the two computers, researchers show that there is nothing mysterious happening: in each individual case, how the button press turns on the light can be explained. Nevertheless, a mystery remains: how does it turn out that the randomly generated stream produced by pressing button alpha always results in the red lamp lighting up? And why does modifying it almost invariably light up the amber lamp? Clearly, there must be some pattern in the 10,000 bit streams, but what is it? While each individual button press and lamp lighting can be explained, we are no closer to understanding the overall pattern that led to the puzzlement in the first place.

The investigators remain stymied until two hackers, who created the boxes, show up. Box A was made by Al, an American who worked for years on expert systems that required him to assemble a database of everyday facts about the world. Everyday facts include things like: elephants are larger than mice; cars move; three is bigger than two; Toronto is a city. Box B was made by Bo, who, working in Swedish, had produced a similar world-knowledge database for his own system. They had got together, added a cable and a translation module, and programmed the boxes so that box A transmits random facts about the world—true ones, if button alpha is pressed, and false ones, if button beta is pressed—while box B uses its own database to evaluate the truth or falsity of the received fact and lights the red lamp if it is true and the green lamp if it is false. If the stream is not a valid sentence, the amber light comes on. Since Al and Bo lived in the same world, they agreed on the truth of the vast majority of facts about the world, so the correlation of alpha to red and beta to green is almost perfect. Modifications to the stream inevitably lead to something that is not a valid sentence.

The mystery is now solved! The causal regularity is based on a semantic feature: the truth or falsity of the interpreted stream of bits. Actually, to be more precise, it is what the boxes consider to be true or false—their "beliefs"?—that explain the causal pattern. In any case, it is only on the intentional level, the semantic level, that any account of the overall pattern can be given. So semantic entities on the intentional level, though attributed from a stance, pick out a real pattern, even by the hardnosed criterion of causal efficacy. As Dennett puts it:

The point of the fable is simple. There is no substitute for the intentional stance; either you adopt it, and explain the pattern by finding the semantic-level facts, or you will forever be baffled by the regularity—the *causal* regularity—that is manifestly there. The same moral, we have seen, can be drawn about interpreting the historical facts of evolutionary history. Even if you can describe, in matchless microdetail, every causal factor in the history of every giraffe who has ever lived, unless you go up a level or two and ask "Why?"—hunting for the *reasons* endorsed by Mother Nature—you will never be able to *explain* the manifest regularities, such as the fact that giraffes have come to have long necks, for instance. (DDI 421)

REALISM

Can we conclude, then, that Dennett is a realist? He is not an industrial strength realist who maintains the "in-itself" reality of intentional objects like beliefs, of design objects like functions, or perhaps even of physical objects like atoms. Each stance picks out one of many possible patterns for its predictive strategy. Some may call this position interpretationism or instrumentalism, others realism. Dennett himself thinks that his position itself is clearer than either label, so he is reluctant to choose. If forced to, he calls his position a "mild and intermediate kind of realism," or a "semi-realism."

This may be a satisfactory answer about the reality of beliefs and functions, which are stance-dependent. Yet Dennett holds that the stances can be successful strategies only because there are patterns in the world that are real. What does it mean to say of patterns themselves that they are real? He is clear that such patterns are only *discernible* from a stance, but do they *exist* independently of stances, that is, prior to being discerned? Do they have a kind of brute existence? Have they been waiting out there from all eternity, as it were, ready to guarantee the success of a stance if it were to arise? Alternatively, is discernibility-in-principle a defining characteristic of patterns of any kind? If a pattern is an informational structure, does its reality depend upon there being some interest in information? If so, is there a kind of super-stance beyond Dennett's three stances, an informational strategy that approaches the universe with an interest in finding patterns, in finding information? Does the notion of pattern itself have an ineliminable reference to the *possibility* of recognition? If so, this position might finally place Dennett on the side of idealism—or at least of antirealism.

Dennett distinguishes between metaphysical and scientific discussions about realism. Philosophers debate in general terms whether any abstract objects are real, as opposed to being unreal, illusory, or fictional. From a scientific point of view, the important distinction is between concepts that are real and those that are bogus. We can define the concept "Dennett's lost sock center" as the geometric center of the smallest sphere that encompasses all his lost socks. In a metaphysical sense, this concept has the same status as a center of gravity: as abstract entities, a philosopher might declare them both equally real or nonreal. Centers of gravity, however, are integrated into a useful mathematical theory that allows us to predict and control the world. The sock center is a *bogus* concept: it fits into no theory that can be used to explain anything. Whatever their metaphysical status, centers of gravity are scientifically "real" while the sock center is bogus, unreal. The question of whether a pattern is a reality-in-itself is like the question of whether a tree falling in the forest makes a noise if there is no one to hear: it is a metaphysical question that doesn't interest him. Dennett's concern is not the mode of being of entities from a philosopher's God's-eye view, but the pragmatic issue of which stances and concepts are available to us in practical terms for dealing with the world. As usual, Dennett prefers to duck the ultimate metaphysical questions and focus instead on scientific realism: for all practical, heuristic purposes patterns are real and it is this reality that accounts for the success of the various stances. What Dennett actually says is that:

> We may be able to make some extended, or metaphorical, sense of the idea of indiscernible patterns (or invisible pictures or silent symphonies), but in the root case a pattern is "by definition" a candidate for pattern *recognition*. (It is this loose but unbreakable link to observers or perspectives, of course, that makes "pattern" an attractive term to someone perched between instrumentalism and industrial strength Realism.) (BC 100)

* * *

Dennett's ontology retrospectively improves our understanding of his positions on mind and evolution. The nature of species and the status of evolved functions can be seen as based on design stance patterns. The contextual nature of conscious states is clearer if we understand them as mildly real entities attributed from the intentional stance rather than as strongly real, self-defining objects such as the intrinsic qualia that qualophiles propose. The debate about whether the attributed rather than substantial status of the self makes it real or fictional can be better understood once we grasp Dennett's position of intermediate realism. His position on each of these issues finds a firmer foundation in his general theory about the nature of reality. The same general theoretical position allows him to integrate humanistic concepts like freedom and ethics into his scientific worldview, as we will see in the next couple of chapters.

CHAPTER 7

FREEDOM: WHAT IS WORTH HAVING?

Is free will an illusion? Dennett's discussion of ontology should warn us against expecting a simple yes or no answer. If reality depends on stances, a more nuanced question is whether there is any stance that reveals freedom as real. His answer is yes: from the intentional stance free will is as real as the self, as reason, and as responsibility—realities it is intimately connected with. Those materialists who maintain that freedom is a fiction have a one-dimensional understanding of ontology and, believing that the physical stance is the only way of adjudicating reality, hold that free will is incompatible with physical determinism and therefore an illusion. Properly understood, claims Dennett, free will is real; understanding it properly, however, requires that we strip from the concept various mythological elements that have misled us.

For an analogy, Dennett offers us romantic love. Some have thought of falling in love as due to Cupid's arrow. A demythologizer who denies the existence of Cupid might be castigated for overthrowing love: is he not declaring love to be an illusion, a fiction? Yet our demythologizer is not denying the reality of love; he is saying that romantic love is real and valuable, but that it is not exactly what some people think it is. Similarly, a successful defence of the reality of free will requires us to jettison various metaphysical components that some philosophers associate with the concept. As Dennett puts it:

> My task will be to . . . provide a unified, stable, empirically well-grounded, coherent view of human free will, and you already know the conclusion I will reach: Free will is real, but it is not a preexisting feature of our existence, like the laws of gravity. It is

also not what tradition declares it to be: a God-like power to exempt oneself from the causal fabric of the physical world. It is an evolved creation of human activity and beliefs, and it is just as real as such other human creations as music and money. And even more valuable. (FE 13)

We will first look at how Dennett's conception of free will as self-control undermines the traditional metaphysical standoff between free will and determinism. Then we will examine his evolutionary account of freedom and his integration of the concept with the notions of reason and responsibility.

FREE WILL

It is the self that is free. As we have seen, for Dennett, the self is a constructed entity whose reality is revealed only by the intentional stance. In particular, states of the self, such as beliefs, are attributed within this stance on the basis of the predictive success of the strategy. The crucial feature of responsibility, however, cannot be attributed to a self unless it is free. Without freedom, would ethics and human values, and the free pursuit of truth by scientists, not be impossible?

First, we need to narrow down the concept of freedom involved. Freedom is defined primarily by contrast, by the kind of obstacle that it is opposed to. The obstacle for political freedom is coercion: to be free in a political sense is not to be coerced by other people or by laws and institutions. The freedom we are concerned with here is not political freedom, but free will, which is contrasted with its purported obstacle: determinism.

Physical determinism is the claim that all things in nature behave according to inviolable and unchanging laws of nature. The 18th century thinker, Laplace, claimed that if we knew all the laws of nature, and the initial conditions, we could in principle predict the occurrence of any material event at any time in the future. This belief in determinism is at the very core of the modern scientific worldview: if we didn't think the universe were governed by laws, there would be little point in pursuing science. (Note that appeal to quantum indeterminism in no way undermines causal determinism in this sense—the sun is still determined to rise in the east! Even if microparticles obey probabilistic laws, the laws of chemistry, of neurophysiology and so on remain as "deterministic" as ever. Laplace would be quite satisfied to use these laws to predict all macroscopic events.)

Physical determinism has been held by many to be incompatible with free will (or "freedom"—I will use the terms interchangeably): either we are material, hence determined, beings and so unfree; or we are free and hence cannot be material beings. Traditionally, materialists have opted for the first horn of the dilemma and denied free will. Descartes and other dualists chose the second horn and declared that since we are free—indeed as free as God, since even God could not deceive us about the *cogito*—the mind must be immaterial, beyond physical nature and its causal laws.

Dennett chooses neither horn of this dilemma. He proposes that freedom and determinism are compatible. A naturalist can accept the materialist worldview and still have freedom, or at least some kinds of freedom. Dennett's aim is to show that our initial fear that freedom and determinism are incompatible is a mistake based on our confusion about what kinds of freedom are worth having. When we analyze in concrete detail the actual things we want when we say we want "freedom," we will discover that not only are they compatible with determinism, but that determinism is a necessary condition for us having them.

SELF-CONTROL

So what do we want when we value our "freedom"? We want a number of things, says Dennett, and we have various fears—bugbears—that determinism means we can't have them. Yet when we look at these fears in the face, they evaporate. Dennett claims that we want self-control; we want to be rational—to be able to govern our conduct by reasons; we want our deliberations to influence our actions; and we want to be able to avoid evil, to be able to "make a difference" and not be forever faced with the inevitable. Each of these is an aspect of freedom. We'll look at each in turn, and see that we can have them all, and determinism too.

Otto is a protagonist who wants to defend freedom, but believes it is incompatible with determinism. Otto argues, "Above all, being free means being in control of ourselves. But self-control is impossible if we are causally determined." This argument is based on a confused notion of control, says Dennett, so we need to analyze the concept.

Control is for an agent with a goal to use some other entity to help achieve that goal. Consider a typical use of the term. NASA can use a radio unit to remotely control a Viking spacecraft and so can force it, like a puppet, to carry out the controllers' purposes. If the spacecraft is going to travel out of effective radio range, however, NASA would be wise to install a computer so that the spacecraft controls itself. It then acts not as a puppet, but as a robot. For it to do so, NASA must design it so that it tends toward some goal, e.g., exploring Mars, and must give it the information it needs to do so, or else the means to get that information. So designed, the spacecraft becomes a "self-controller."

It is possible that either the remote control system or the self-control system might break down. In that case the spacecraft would be "out of control," that is, it would then be incapable of carrying out either the objectives of the remote controller or its own internally programmed goals. If it crashes into Mars under the force of gravity, whatever information it would have in its data banks about goals and how to achieve them would be irrelevant to its behavior.

The central point of Dennett's argument is that, in all three situations, the spacecraft is determined by physical laws. Control and self-control are possible only because of physical processes, and even in the case of not behaving toward a goal, that is, of being out of control, the spacecraft is still physically determined.

Consider another example: in a game of billiards we try to control the ball, but in roulette if someone effectively controls the ball (with a magnet?) we feel cheated. In roulette, the ball is supposed to be uncontrolled. Yet no one thinks that the roulette ball thereby escapes the laws of nature. Knowing that the roulette table is fully subject to deterministic laws still does not tell us whether it is controlled or not.

The conclusion is that *"determinism does not in itself 'erode control'"* (ER 72). Far from being incompatible with causation, control, self-control, and even being out of control are all possible only because of physical determinism; they are all modes of being determined.

In the case of selves, what we want is to be self-controlled. We have goals and we attempt to achieve them by searching out the information we need to accomplish them. Many things are incompatible with self-control: We rightly fear control by others: military dictators, torturers, brainwashers, TV commercials, neurologists with brain probes, subliminal hypnotists, or evil demons. Many of us worry about getting out of control, of losing control of our-selves; Lou Gehrig's disease, MS, or Alzheimer's come to mind as extreme cases. These are real dangers to our self-control; determin-ism is not.

"But," objects Otto, "surely if determinism is true, then we are controlled by our environment?"

Dennett considers this fear, this bugbear, to be based on false personification. "The environment, not being an agent, does not control us" (ER 61). If a NASA spacecraft crashes on Mars under the force of gravity, the problem is not that it is being controlled by physical laws; it is simply uncontrolled. Nature is not an agent, not a self; it has no desires for us; it doesn't make us do what it wants, for it has no wants. We may cease to be self-controlled and go out of control, but that doesn't mean we fall into the clutches of some Laplacean demon and become other-controlled. If I am out of control, then there is no coherent purpose, my own or anyone else's, to my behavior. There is not a simple dichotomy between self-control and determinism. Otto needs a more elabo-rate conceptual scheme. He is wrong to think that what is not self-controlled is other-controlled; there is a third alternative: being out of control. And so determinism is not incompatible with free-dom as self-control.

Even if this argument is correct, Otto has other worries. Following the lead of Descartes, he claims that freedom is the capacity to act rationally, to be guided by reasons, or—what amounts to the same thing—to do things for a purpose, to act in view of the good (as one sees it). Yet for Descartes, there is a rigid contrast between being caused to do something—being determined by an external force, as he would put it—and doing something for a reason. The mate-rial world is governed by causes, the mind by reasons. Free beings direct themselves toward the (or their) good while material nature is blind to all value. To be free is to be directed by reasons, but rea-sons are not conditions of the physical world, hence it would seem that exemption of one's mind from physical determinism is the only hope for having a rational will.

Dennett has already offered us (in Chapter 4) an evolutionary, naturalistic account of how acting for a reason fits into the natu-ral, causal scheme. Once there were no reasons, only causes. Then organisms came to respond to things in their environment not just by reacting to their objective physical properties, but by categorizing them from the viewpoint of the organism's interests and acting accordingly. This was the birth of free-floating rationales. Organisms came to respond to the informational features of the world, the "meaning" the things had for the organism, not just to their brute physical properties. Gravity acts on a planet without regard for any purpose or interest of the planet: it has none. In contrast, how a stimulus affects an organism depends not just on the physical nature of the stimulus, but on the goals of the organism, on its history, and so on the information it has. Whether a cell absorbs a molecule of sugar depends not just on the sugar, but on the goal of the cell, whether it "needs" more sugar right now or not, which in turn depends on when it last "ate." This is not a violation of causality, but a way of structuring causation so as to subordinate it to the design of the organism, to organic teleology. That's what a design is: a way of structuring causation.

A mouse, for instance, responds with similar evasive action to the spring of a cat or the swoop of an eagle not because they have anything in common from the physical stance, but because both are categorized as "predators" from the mouse's point of view. They both carry the same information for the mouse: time you were out of here! Given the mouse's interest in survival, there are reasons to act in one way rather than another. That is, the mouse's action is purposeful and guided by information.

It is clear from such cases that acting for reasons is not opposed to, or incompatible with, being moved by physical forces. To act for a reason is to allow a physical cause to influence the organism only "with respect"; it involves a kind of delayed reaction. Far from reason and causation being in opposition, acting for a reason is only possible in a causally deterministic world.

"But," objects Otto, "what about the uniqueness of human beings?" Does Dennett's position not grant freedom to all organisms, even single cell organisms? Is this not a reductio ad absurdum of the materialist's account of freedom?

Far from being a reductio, maintaining that primitive organisms already act on the basis of free-floating rationales is indicative of Dennett's gradualism. He is very suspicious of all-or-nothing theories. Unlike Descartes, he doesn't think that a being is either totally free or else totally unfree. Primitive organisms act to some extent on the basis of information, and so they are more "free" than, say, planets. They have a kind of "proto-freedom." Freedom must evolve from somewhere, so any black-and-white theories that make such development impossible must be wrong.

Nevertheless, Dennett holds that human beings are unique in that we are capable of knowing the reasons we act for. We go beyond free-floating rationales to reflective reasons. We not only form representations of things in the world; we also represent to ourselves our goals and our reasons, by means of language or other symbols. That is what makes us selves. Just as categorization of the physical world gives the primitive organism a certain control over brute causation, so reflective consciousness based on language gives us some leverage over our own goals.

Yet the basic analysis is the same. To act for a reason, whether the reason is a free-floating rationale or is represented to oneself, is not to go against determinism, but to structure causal processes in a way that contributes to our interests, that allows us to act for our good. Freedom is acting rationally on the basis of information, so it is not only compatible with causation, it is one particular structure or mode of causation.

Otto still objects. To be able to act on the basis of reflection requires that, as selves, we deliberate about possible goals and courses of action; but if we are determined, Laplace's demon can calculate what we are going to do next, so what is the point of deliberating? Deliberation would seem to have no place in the natural, causal order; it is at most an epiphenomenal process—one that has no effect on the world—that we are forced to perform. Hence freedom is still incompatible with determinism.

Dennett responds by analyzing the difference between Laplacean calculation and deliberation by a self. From the viewpoint of Laplace's demon, any future state of the universe can be predicted by calculation: all that is needed is to calculate the future state of every particle in the universe at that future time. Note that there are no shortcuts; it won't do to calculate only particles on the earth, since we need to ensure that no comet will collide with the earth during the time we're considering. Only an almost infinite, probably divine, calculator could possibly handle the computations needed to say what will happen in this room five minutes from now. What is a poor finite human creature with time restraints to do?

Deliberate! Unlike calculation, deliberation is a heuristic process by which an organism uses quick and dirty methods to get a rough estimation of what is likely to happen in its vicinity on the basis of the limited information available to it. Only a few factors are considered: those that are likely to be relevant. Only macroscopic agglomerations enter into consideration. Rough approximations rather than exact calculations speed up the process. Within a fraction of a second I can estimate the state of this room five minutes from now. Of course, my estimate won't be certain, nor exact, but how else could we finite beings be expected to get along in the world? Better to act now after a brief heuristic deliberation and perhaps get it wrong than to sit calculating for centuries after the moment has passed!

"So what?" says Otto. Does this not miss the point? In a deterministic world what is the use of deliberating, heuristically or otherwise? Is the outcome not already decided by fate? Indeed, are not the steps in the deliberation themselves already predestined?

No, says Dennett, this is to confuse determinism with fatalism, with inevitability. Consider a genuine instance of fatalism: if Otto is sucked out the faulty window of a plane, he has about three minutes while he is falling to the ground to deliberate philosophically about what he should do. But this is futile, as Otto correctly sees. What is about to happen cannot be the result of, will not be influenced by, his deliberations. On the other hand, when Dennett reserved his seat, he *did* deliberate about the safety of Wing-and-a-Prayer Airlines, checked his Consumer Reports (the best heuristic method he could think of) chose a different airline and so arrived safely. Buying the ticket he did was a real (causal) result of his deliberations. This is not fatalistic: Dennett's deliberations made a difference—and Otto's would have too, if he had deliberated.

Determinism is not fatalism. In a deterministic world, we can still distinguish between those events that, though determined, are the result of deliberation and those that are determined in a simple, informationally insensitive way. Otto is confused: what he really fears is fatalism, not determinism. What we want is that as many events in our lives as possible not be subject to fate, but be events that we can deliberate about in a manner that is effective. And Dennett is an optimist: while he grants that "there are indeed conditions under which deliberation is futile . . . [I]t is our good fortune that these conditions are abnormal in our world" (ER 106). What we want is that our deliberations be effective; and in our deterministic world they often are.

But Otto is determined and insists that Dennett is still missing the point. Deliberation is a pure farce, for if determinism is true, then the events that are going to happen to us are inevitable, unavoidable, and so there is no freedom.

Dennett claims we must analyze the notions of "avoidable" and "inevitable" more carefully before acquiescing in this argument. Suppose astronomers discover a comet that is about to crash into the earth and cause a major disaster. At the last moment another comet, previously unnoticed by astronomers, appears in just the right place to prevent the first from hitting the earth and so the catastrophe is avoided. "The" catastrophe? There was never going to be one! The second comet has been on track from all eternity, so the collision was never in the cards.

From the Laplacean point of view nothing could ever be prevented, so from this perspective it would be meaningless to distinguish the avoidable from the inevitable. Prevention, inevitability, and avoidance only make sense to a finite actor, an agent who has to make heuristic predictions and develop expectations on the basis of limited information. It is when these expected events do not occur due to the actions of a deliberator that we speak of avoidance.

> Against the background of that anticipated future (that misanticipated future) we see the events that happen as an instance of prevention. . . . All the verbs of "making a difference" ["prevent," "avoid," "expect," "bring about," "thwart," "disturb the universe"] involve a tacit comparison between the way the world was *apparently* going to go and the way it turned out to go. (ER 125–126)

Unlike Laplace's demon, finite deliberators live in a world structured by their own categories. We don't live in a world of microparticles; we live in a world of trees and birds, of exams that are passed, and wars that break out. As intentional beings, as selves, we classify events in terms of whether our deliberate action can make a difference. The sun will rise tomorrow no matter what I do; that is inevitable. Failing my exam is avoidable, for I can decide to study for it and thereby prevent the "normal," heuristically expected outcome from occurring. Such distinctions make sense only from our macro point of view, from the pragmatic perspective of a human self with limited information, that is, from the intentional stance.

They differentiate events that happen as a result of deliberation from those with causal chains that do not pass through deliberation. If we as finite deliberators are to be efficient, we must clearly distinguish between those situations where the expected outcomes are avoidable, and so are worth deliberating about, and those situations that are "inevitable."

Imagine someone arguing, "Since determinism is true, thermostats don't control temperature," or "Since determinism is true, planets would move in ellipses even if there were no gravity." Determinism "works through" the thermostat; it works via gravity. In a similar way, Dennett is claiming, it can work through deliberation. A causal sequence that does not pass through the self's deliberative process we label "inevitable"; if it passes through deliberation, we call it "preventable" or "avoidable." Hence "inevitable" doesn't mean the same as "determined," and "avoidable" doesn't mean "nondetermined."

So Otto is incorrect in saying that if determinism is true then all events are inevitable. He is confusing categories from the physical stance with intentional ones. Some events (though determined) involve deliberation, and it is with respect to these events that we can act freely and "make a difference."

FREEDOM WORTH HAVING

Otto still wants more: in the end, when I long for freedom what I want is that, whatever choice I make, I feel I could have done otherwise. More—since feelings can be mistaken—I want to actually have the capacity to have done otherwise. Is freedom not, finally, the arbitrary ability to spontaneously and unpredictably do whatever I do, knowing that I could have done otherwise? "That's what I want," insists Otto.

"Really?" asks Dennett. "Are you sure that's what you want?" For instance, if I am faced with a difficult philosophical objection, do I really want to have the arbitrary choice of killing or not killing the objector? If I thought for one moment that I could do a thing like that, I for one (Dennett for another) would be devastated. I know there are thugs on the streets of some cities who could kill you if you objected to the color of their jacket; they are governed by their impulses and their decisions are close to arbitrary. Yet is that freedom? When my parents brought me up, they worked hard to make me into the kind of self who could not act like that, and since I took over my own rearing, I've been trying to achieve the same thing. I want my actions to be guided by reasons, to head in the direction that goodness points. In becoming a certain kind of self, my actions reflect my history and values; they are mine in the sense of flowing from who I have become, from the narrative I give myself. If arbitrariness is what Otto ultimately means by freedom, then I don't want it (and I hope he doesn't get it!) That kind of freedom is not worth having.

Otto responds: "What about all those times I lay awake at night with guilt, tormenting myself with the question of whether I could have done otherwise? Was this useless? Are you suggesting I could have avoided all that suffering?"

Not entirely, thinks Dennett. If Otto was trying to change the past, yes, it was totally useless, probably neurotic: what is done is done; he cannot now undo it. But a more charitable interpretation is to see Otto not as trying to change the past, but as trying to change the future. According to Dennett, this is what most of us who ask ourselves, "Could I have done otherwise?" have in mind. It is not that I am asking some metaphysical question about the status of alternative possible decisions in the past. It is that I want to learn from my experience. This particular event may no longer be under my control, since it is past. Yet it is worth considering whether future events that are similar in some relevant way might be controlled differently. Are there some factors that I left out of my deliberations in the past that I should remind myself to include in the future? Lying awake asking whether I could have done otherwise is usually an attempt to rationally reconsider my policies, to reprogram myself so that in similar circumstances in the future I will act differently.

Consider again the scenario of the Viking spacecraft. Freed from NASA control, it is under its own self-control. Its information sensors tell it it is off course, so it corrects its heading. We can imagine a spacecraft with a learning program sophisticated enough to go further and investigate why it went off course. An investigation like that could lead to one of two conclusions. One possibility is that it might find that the course deviation had been due to a meteorite collision of a kind that its computer systems are powerless to predict. At this stage, it terminates the investigation with the conclusion, "couldn't have done otherwise." That is, there is nothing to be learned about future policies. An alternative conclusion might be that the deviation was caused by the gravitational effect of Mars' moons, which the spacecraft is capable of calculating, but it had not been programmed to do so. The conclusion is that it "could have done otherwise" and so it reprograms itself to take such factors into account in the future. The aim of such investigation is neither to leave the spacecraft racked with guilt, nor to have it ponder the metaphysical question of whether it could have done otherwise in the past, but simply the practical, strategic goal of improving its behavior in the future.

> The conscience that manifests itself only retrospectively in agonies of remorse, and never prospectively in overcoming some base urge, is a singularly unattractive trait of character, and one that any moral world could well do without. The sort of remorse that (on the other hand) is a manifestation of some significant, projectible, nonmomentary shift in priorities for decision is precisely the sort of attitude the institution of holding people responsible exists to achieve. So that sort of remorse has an entirely appropriate place in our naturalized institution of guilt. (ER 167)

So freedom as "the ability to have done otherwise," could simply refer to the capacity to learn from past mistakes and adjust our behavior in the future. Such freedom is valuable; indeed, it is the very essence of narrative selfhood: the central characteristic of a historical self is that its past influences its future. But if the phrase is given a metaphysical interpretation, then it offers us a mystifying vision of a freedom we don't have. It is also a freedom that we would not want if we could have it. It is a freedom not worth having.

Dennett concludes that, if we relinquish metaphysical abstractions, the kinds of freedom that a real, practical self acting in this world would want are freedoms that are not compromised by determinism. His intentional understanding of the self allows us to have our cake and eat it too. If he's right, we can accept naturalism and brain-based minds without having to give up freedom and dignity. The hardware of the brain may be governed by deterministic laws revealed by the physical stance, yet on the level of the intentional stance, we can still respond to reasons, and so we can still be self-controllers who deliberate effectively, act purposefully, pursue the good, avoid the avoidable, and even reprogram ourselves on the basis of experience. That is real freedom, the only kind worth having. And it is available to us not in spite of our being determined, but precisely because we are determined.

EVOLUTION OF FREEDOM

Putting to rest the metaphysical bugbears allows Dennett to give us a naturalist account of practical, heuristic freedom: freedom is self-control; freedom is information-sensitive behavior; freedom is response to factors categorized by the interests of the organism; freedom is acting for a reason. All of these characterizations amount to the same thing and are to be found to some extent in every organism. Human freedom evolves gradually from the (proto-)freedom that precedes it, so we should not expect all-or-nothing leaps from unfreedom to freedom. The gradual evolution of freedom parallels the evolution of reason, of meaning, and of selfhood since these concepts go hand in hand within the design and intentional stances.

Nevertheless, human freedom goes beyond proto-freedom, just as reflective reasons transcend free-floating rationales even as they develop out of them. The arrival of language is the central factor in the transition to distinctively human freedom. Language, and the social communication that comes with it, force us to reflect on and evaluate our motives, to discuss the rationality of our desires, and so allows us a certain degree of freedom with respect to the construction of our selves. With language, we gain some freedom with respect to our internal environment, not only about actions in the world. Linguistically transmitted memes offer us alternative reasons for action, so we can adopt new values for our lives. The construction of narrative selves creates a new center for control: control by the self. It is the integration of reflective reasons for action into the narratively organized self that makes human freedom distinctive.

This is not to pit human freedom against biology: biological evolution sets up the framework within which freedom is constructed. Culture, self, and freedom are not opposed to biology; they are possibilities opened up by it. It is our genetic inheritance that makes them possible; genes accomplish their objectives through our cultural constructs, just as physical determinism works through control and self-control. There should be no standoff between those who believe that humans act on the basis of their thinking and those who believe in genetic influence ("My genes made me do it!").

Yet biology is not enough. Language is fundamental to reflective reason and to free will. A free human action—as opposed to the proto-freedom of other organisms—is one we can give a reason for, to others or to ourselves. As Dennett puts it:

> We can ask each other to do things, and we can ask ourselves to do things. . . . We can engage in the practice of asking, and giving, reasons. . . . It is this kind of asking, which we can also direct to ourselves, that creates the special category of voluntary actions that sets us apart. . . . They result from decisions we make in the course of trying to make sense of ourselves and our own lives. (FE 251)

* * *

A voluntary action is one I am responsible for. It is an action that has been filtered through that mode of organization called a self. It is an action that is based on who I am, on who I have become. It is an action that I can account for on the basis of my knowledge and values. It is an action I can give a reason for, a reason that I can express in language to myself, or to others. In the face of danger, a soldier, like a bird, might automatically and "naturally" flee, but if the soldier has been telling himself a story about his own bravery, if his history has led him to value patriotism, then he may choose to stand his ground: a clear case of freedom as control by the self.

A crucial part of any such story is the meme for freedom itself. The soldier has not only been infected by the memes for bravery and patriotism, but above all he has taken on the meme for free will. The notion that a self can determine its own actions in accord with its own values is a meme definitive of selfhood. Could one have free will if one believed one did not? Dennett holds that believing oneself to be free is a necessary condition for freedom. This implies that freedom is fragile: what has been constructed can be destroyed. It is held in place by cultural institutions and individual beliefs and if these were to be undermined, free will itself could disappear. Since Dennett holds freedom to be highly valuable, he views his own arguments as attempts to give it a firm foundation without which there is a danger of free will vanishing once and for all.

He is therefore distressed when others have interpreted his position as claiming that free will is an illusion.

> . . . [N]o, free will is *not* an illusion; all the varieties of free will worth wanting are, or can be, ours—but you have to give up a bit of false and outdated ideology to understand how this can be so. Romantic love minus Cupid's arrow is still worth yearning for. It is still, indeed, romantic love, real romantic love. (FE 224–225)

> Human freedom is not an illusion; it is an objective phenomenon. . . . Human freedom is real—as real as language, music and money—so it can be studied objectively from a no-nonsense, scientific point of view. But like language, music, money, and other products of society, its persistence is affected by what we believe about it. (FE 305)

It is true that freedom does not exist in its own right, like gravity or the moon; it exists as a social construct that persists in its being only with our support. It is among our most valuable creations, one that we should act to preserve. Giving it a firm, naturalistic foundation within the scientific worldview is one of the most important steps in preserving it.

> My own intuition pumps are designed to help. Yes, if we try hard, we can imagine a being that listens to the voice of reason and yet is not exempted from the causal milieu. Yes, we can imagine a being whose every decision is caused by the interaction of features of its current state and features of its environment over which it has no control—and yet which is itself *in control*, and not being controlled by that omnipresent and omnicausal environment. Yes, we can imagine a process of self-creation that starts with a nonresponsible agent and builds, gradually, to an agent responsible for its own character. Yes, we can imagine a rational *and deterministic* being who is not deluded when it views its future as open and "up to" it. Yes, we can imagine a responsible, free agent of whom it is true that whenever it acted in the past, it could not have acted otherwise. (ER 170)

Only with a free self, responsible for its own actions, can we find a basis for ethics and morality, the subject of our next chapter.

CHAPTER 8

ETHICS AND RELIGION:
EVOLUTION AND BEYOND

Freedom, we have seen, is not threatened by the scientific world-view, but what about other human values? Human dignity in general, many think, is being encroached upon by science and needs defending. Dennett agrees. The sacred value of human life is fragile and can be held in place only by a suitable global belief environment to support it. Religion may seem to supply the requisite belief environment by promulgating the myth of a spiritual soul—the noble lie. Dennett thinks this is an unsuitable foundation, for it is bound to fail in the long run.

> Doesn't the very meaning of our lives depend on the reality of our immaterial souls? No. We don't need to be made of two fundamentally different kinds of substance, matter and mind-stuff, to have morally meaningful lives. On the face of it, the idea that all our striving and loving, our yearning and regretting, our hopes and fears, depend on some secret ingredient, some science-proof nugget of specialness that defies the laws of nature, is an almost childish ploy: "Let's gather up all the wonderfulness of human life and sweep it into the special hidey-hole where science can never get at it!" (PHD)

The alternative is to find a solid foundation for morality and human value within naturalism. This is not a vain hope: the evolving cooperative social nature of the human species has given rise to ethics and religion and it is from the perspective of this evolution that we can come to understand and evaluate them. I'll start with Dennett's treatment of ethics, and then move on to religion.

ETHICS

Ethical values are central to human dignity, but how are we to understand them within naturalism? The heuristic nature of evolutionary situations challenges traditional philosophical theories of ethics by offering an alternative theory based on the necessary conditions for group cooperation. While some worry that sociobiological approaches undermine distinctively human values, we will see that this concern is based on a misunderstanding. In fact, the evolution of selfhood and responsibility leads to the creation of new centers of value that offer us a solid foundation not only for morality but for the sacredness of life, for the claim that life is meaningful and worth living.

The foundation of morality, according to traditional philosophical accounts, is based on absolute ideals. Plato held that there are eternal forms that set the standards for goodness in human life, action, and society. Kantian ethics is based on the self-legislating judgements of an autonomous, rational subject purified from desire, interest, and selfishness—an ideal, if ever there was one. Utilitarians determine what is right or wrong on the basis of an ideal hedonic calculation of the greatest good for the greatest number in the long run, all factors considered.

Heuristics

As attempts to find abstract justifications for morality, such philosophical theories have an important role, but as realistic techniques for decision-making in practical life they are typically of little help, as anyone who has tried to apply them to everyday problems knows all too well. In a real situation, which of many ideal Platonic forms are to be applied, or which self-legislated maxim is to be followed? In practice, it is impossible to consider all factors: there simply is no time.

Dennett offers an illustration of these difficulties: on the basis of a philanthropic grant, a philosophy department advertises nationally a massive scholarship for the most promising philosophy student. Unexpectedly, it receives hundreds of thousands of detailed applications with CVs, writing samples, and reference letters. Careful examination of each application is impossible before the deadline, so what is to be done? Considering the criteria for the ideal philosophy student, the rights of each individual, or the happiness of the greatest number is impracticable. Obviously some quick and dirty method must be used to winnow down the numbers. The selection committee is forced to rely on marks, grade point averages, or number of philosophy courses, although everyone realizes that these are poor indicators of "the most promising philosophy student." After this initial cut, perhaps they can examine in more detail the remaining ten or a hundred applications.

So we see that, in the real world decision-making requires time-constrained, heuristic methods rather than the pure, rational application of absolute principles. As Dennett puts it, while waiting for the Doctor of Philosophy to arrive, we must rely on the Moral First Aid Manual.

Evolution of ethics

Similarly in evolution, given the time constraints of biological situations, it is something more like Moral First Aid that has developed in humans, rather than dependence on the ideal or absolute norms proposed by moral philosophers. Human beings are a highly social species and the evolution of cooperation required the creation of heuristic rules of engagement. It is in these rules, rather than in metaphysics, that we must look for the origin of ethics and human dignity.

Cooperation requires that individuals subordinate their own selfish interests to the interests of the group, that is, be altruistic. So the evolution of ethics might be thought of as the development of pure altruism. Dennett thinks that much insight into this evolution can be discovered in the work of game theorists in economics and related fields.

The aim of the game theoretic approach is to understand the strategic factors involved in interactions, so it hypothesizes a system of agents, agents who are abstract in the sense that whether they are humans, insects, or other organisms is irrelevant. This kind of system can be simulated on a computer to discover the effects of modifying various parameters. Philosophers often speculate on what might happen if everyone were to act on a particular maxim or policy, but game theorists can examine more sophisticated scenarios: What would happen if *some*—a given percentage—acted in one way, while others adopted different strategies?

From this perspective, it seems easy, initially, to account for the evolution of cooperation by pointing to the huge survival advantage of acting as a cooperative group. Think of the group as the unit of survival—those groups that internally cooperate are more adaptive than those groups that don't.

Unfortunately, in simulations of an evolutionary community of cooperative, altruistic agents, the introduction of a freeloader—an agent who accepts all the benefits and resources of the group while not paying the costs—undermines the community, for the defector has a reproductive advantage. Hence, generations later, freeloaders within the group will swamp cooperators. To understand the evolution of such groups we need to explain how cooperative individuals evolve, and, given the survival advantage of selfish individuals, it is hard to see how this can occur. It seems that since selfishness always wins out and altruism is doomed, there can be no evolutionary account for the origin of ethics.

Fortunately, this model is too simple to be realistic. The addition of various complicating factors results in more optimistic scenarios. First, there is the neighborhood effect: if the model is modified to allow agents to choose who they interact with, cooperators tend to form groups among themselves, leaving defectors stuck with each other. Altruism can then thrive in these local groups.

The simulation can be complicated further by granting the agents some longer-term intelligence. Selfish agents may come to see that being nice to others in the short-term will bring long-term benefits. Inspired by Ben Franklin's saying, "We must indeed all hang together, or, most assuredly, we shall all hang separately," Dennett refers to this strategy as "benselfishness." This is not yet pure altruism, but such long-term self-interest is a step along the way.

If the simulated agents are given the capacity to learn from experience, a cooperator may remember which agents have defected in the past and so avoid interactions with them in the future. Further, if we grant some minimal communication, other cooperators may shun the defectors, even though they themselves have not had a bad experience with them. If the cost of punishment is low, according to some computer simulations, such activity enhances the level of cooperation. Particularly effective is the punishment of those who fail to shun violators. Under these modified conditions, cooperative individuals have an evolutionary advantage so the evolution of cooperation and altruism can be understood.

Are we there yet? Does this account for the evolution of ethics? Hardly! A cooperative community like that may be well ordered, but the actions of individual agents are at most cases of enlightened self-interest, of benselfishness, not of what we call morality. They do not treat others as ends-in-themselves. Game theoretic simulations show that the evolution of cooperation is theoretically possible and so may account for the first gradual steps toward morality, but we will need language, culture, and memes to move us further along.

True morality requires a conscious, rational self committed to doing the right thing. A self of this nature is infected with the meme for morality, for performing actions because they are right. It is reflectively aware of its own desires and so has a certain freedom to select its own motivations; and it chooses to do what is good. But how can this work? A reflective person can see the rational advantages of defecting, at least when they can get away with it—when no one is looking, for instance. The idea of a vigilant God who is always looking may reduce this temptation, but doing good only out of fear of God is a very immature morality indeed.

A more promising approach can be found by analyzing the commitment problem. In a culture based on language we commit ourselves verbally to marriage, to paying our debts, to giving a course of lectures, and so on, and—no matter how good our intention—we will get along poorly if others do not trust us. There is actually a double problem here: not only must we have the self-discipline to carry out our commitments; we also need to be able to convince others that we will do so. They must be convinced that we will fulfill our promises even if, when the time comes, it is no longer in our narrow self-interest to do so. Once bluffers—fake cooperators—use language, there is an arms race of concealment strategies and bluff-detection and as a result humans have become extremely good at spotting defectors, though never perfect. Talk is cheap. Anyone can *say* that they are reliable. One can swear on a Bible, but that too can be faked. One can swear on two Bibles. One can swear on a stack of Bibles.

In a society based on language, ironically, words are never enough. The problem is how to bind oneself in the future and do it in a manner that is visible to others. In a famous episode in Homer, Ulysses knows that when he sails by the Sirens he will be seduced, i.e., that it will seem to him in terms of short-term rationality that he should give in to their temptations. So he has his sailors bind him to the mast in order that, when that future moment comes, his will will be ineffective, that is, he will be simply incapable of changing his mind.

The problem, in general terms, is the relation of rationality to time. We discount the future value of things, and so immediate rewards move us more than long-term rewards. Young children choose the offer of one candy immediately over an offer of two candies 15 minutes later. To become a mature self, an adult who is free—free to engage in long-term projects—I must gain enough self-understanding to be able to predict what my future choices are likely to be and then—like Ulysses—when these choices are incompatible with my long-term goals, I must devise tactics to circumvent them. If I am an insightful alcoholic, I may be able to predict that if I enter a bar I will choose to drink too much; so I can achieve my long-term goal of sobriety by choosing not to enter a bar. We have already seen (in Chapter 5) that communicating with oneself over time is one of the defining features of selfhood. To learn to commit oneself is to extend the self so that one identifies less with what one is at the current instant and more with a self that endures over time. Rationality must be extended from short-term to long-term. Yet how is this modification of rationality possible?

Ironically, suggests Dennett, it is emotion that carries me beyond short-term rationality to long-term rationality. I must become passionate about my own integrity and reputation. I must become so emotionally involved in my long-term project that my passion renders me irrational—short-term irrational—when faced with immediate advantages. To say I am committed to a goal is to say that my passion for it would make me irrational in the face of attractive distractions along the way. Because Ulysses is committed to getting home to Ithaca, he does not pursue the obvious good offered by the Sirens along the way. Because I am passionate about my reputation, I repay my debt even when I could get away with not doing so. I threaten an intruder and, even when I come to realize he is bigger than me, my rage leads me to carry out my threat despite the fact that it is no longer wise to do so.

And the intruder, seeing my rage, believes that I really will, irrationally, attack him; that is, he trusts that I will do as I say. This analysis of commitment in terms of emotion, therefore, also solves the second aspect of the commitment problem: convincing others. Passion is visible to others. People can see from my expression, from my tone, from my face, and from my history that I am so passionate about my own integrity and reputation that I will repay the money they are lending me even if it is not in my selfish best interest to do so when the time comes. So they trust me to do what I say I'll do; they believe I will not be a defector.

But maybe I'm deceiving them. Perhaps I am faking it and just putting on a show. Emotions, however, are not easy to control: emotional pretence requires great effort in the long run and, in the end is seldom effective at convincing others. The easiest and most effective way of gaining a reputation for fulfilling one's commitments is actually to do so. The best way to *seem good* is to *be good*. As a result, in the linguistic, social life of humans, there is evolutionary pressure to select those who actually are committed, as opposed to pretending to be. The kind of person who gets beyond selfishness, who lives up to their commitments, who honestly promotes the good of others, and who treats the happiness of others as an end in itself, therefore has, under these conditions, an evolutionary advantage. So Dennett has a possible evolutionary explanation, a Just So story, for the evolution not just of long-term self-interest—benselfishness—but for real morality itself.

Creation of new values

This evolutionary account of the origin of morality has an obvious objection. Since the whole Darwinian theory is based on the principle of survival of the fittest, does biological survival not trump all other values, even those of morality? If so, how could persons ever be ends-in-themselves; how could we ever act for the sake of the good? Is every individual not ultimately driven by the value of survival, if not the individual's own, at least the survival of the species?

For Dennett, this is the kind of greedy reductionism that must be rejected. Humans are not purely biological creatures, so he thinks this fear of genetic determinism is greatly exaggerated. It is true that if the human race became extinct, all human values would perish with it. Yet there is a lot of space between here and there. Human selves are memetic creations; memetic values transcend the biological and endow selves with values other than survival.

Memes, as we have seen (in Chapter 4), are "selfish": they replicate because the memes themselves have, in their particular environment, some survival advantage, an advantage that may—but may not—enhance the survival and reproduction of the individuals or societies involved. Individuals who dedicate themselves to a religious meme may on occasion choose to lay down their own lives in the service of their religion. The Shakers believed in sexual celibacy for all and the whole sect is now, not surprisingly, extinct. Similarly, the meme for war, especially in a nuclear age, could well endanger the survival of the human species. The point about Dennett's memetic theory is that human values transmitted by culture or inherited from history are what characterize human life; they have a measure of autonomy and cannot be reduced to biological survival. Sometimes they improve the chances of biological survival, but sometimes they do not. For Dennett, human values and dignity cannot be reduced to the purely biological.

The mistake, Dennett believes, comes from thinking of Darwinism as a biological theory rather than as an abstract, algorithmic process. We must always ask, "*Cui bono?*"—to whose benefit? The idea of the Selfish Gene, that adaptation is for the benefit of the gene, may be appropriate to prehuman evolution, but once the cultural transmission of memes begins, there are new entities that may benefit. Memes create new answer-candidates for the *cui bono*? question.

Yet does this response not just substitute memetic determinism for genetic determinism? How can there be morality if selves are pushed around by forces beyond themselves, by "principalities and powers"?

This objection slips back into some substantialist misconception of the self as a pre-existing entity that memes, secondarily, act upon. For Dennett, selves are memetic entities through and through; they are creations of memes. A self is not a pure, pre-existing subject—a *cogito*—that secondarily comes to possess cultural goods; it is a cultural being to the core. ". . . [We are] not just guardians and transmitters of culture, but cultural entities ourselves—all the way in" (EE).

An idea does not inhabit a self like a bump in a log; as a responsible entity, a self that has been infected with a meme endorses it personally. If a person absorbs the belief that persons are to be respected as ends-in-themselves, then this is a value that the person subscribes to, a value that partly defines who they are. Such a person has adopted a new value, a value that transcends the biological, a value that makes her an authentically moral being.

One could even say that memes allow selves to get beyond themselves, to transcend their own selfishness. At first sight, memes appear to be as selfish as genes: their own survival is all that counts.

It is true that the notion of survival is inevitably selfish, in a certain way. Yet we need to be careful in interpreting this selfishness. When Dawkins promotes the notion of the selfish gene, his idea is certainly not that genes make individuals selfish. His idea is rather that those genes that code for phenotypes which fail to promote the gene are not likely to survive. The survival of the phenotypic individual as such is a secondary issue. Similarly, the fact that only memes that are capable of replicating themselves survive does not mean that the host individuals act only for their own selfish purposes. A meme for suicide bombing may survive precisely by the nonsurvival of its host; those infected by it do not act selfishly, or only with a mind to their own survival. Memes may result in unselfish, altruistic selves.

Dennett goes even further and suggests that opposing self and other, or selfishness and altruism, is ultimately an inadequate way of thinking about ethics. Economic game theories, selfish genes, or even memes for treating others as ends-in-themselves can give us insight into the origin of ethics, but his account of selfhood, it seems to me, allows him to go further.

It is here that the strength of Dennett's theory of the self comes to fruition. If the self is thought of as a substance, an isolated island, then the problem of morality gets interpreted as the task of explaining altruism: how can an essentially selfish ego come to value others? Conceiving of the self as a mode of organization spread over space and time, on the other hand, allows it to extend dynamically over space and time. Extending itself in time, so that it identifies with itself in the future, accounts for commitment. Extending itself in space involves identifying itself with family member, tribal groups, sports teams, nations, or even humanity as a whole. A member of a sports team does not face a problem of overcoming selfishness and becoming altruistic: if anything, the threat they face is loss of their selfhood in group hysteria. More positively, they treat other team members as components of their own selfhood; they have an extended self. In a team situation, we do not have isolated substantial selves struggling to implement moral maxims—treat others as ends-in-themselves, do unto others as you would have them do onto you, etc. Rather, we have selves with fluid modes of organization that incorporate others in their identity. Just as the brain, to take an analogy, is not obsessed only with its own survival, but acts for the survival of the whole individual, it is possible that each person, as part of the body-politic, has a mode of organization—a self—that incorporates others within its group. This is what we mean when we speak about a person's "identity": insofar as they identify with their community, their "selfish" concern may extend to cover others in their group. Those who identify with a sports team experience the team as an extended "self," so that acting "selfishly" requires them to subordinate their own individual desires for the good of the team. The narrow "I" has become a broad "we."

If this interpretation is correct, then Dennett's notion of the extended self allows him to unify his accounts of the evolution of selfhood and the origin of morality. A responsible self is a mode of organization created through linguistic communication with others—and the arms race that this communication brings about. The result is a self capable of committing itself to others, and to norms beyond itself, that is, to morality. The good of others is not an add-on: it is constitutive of selfhood.

Summary so far

Dennett's account of ethics is, therefore, tightly integrated with his theory of a responsible self constructed by gradual genetic, and later memetic, evolution. He eschews metaphysical, absolutist approaches to ethics and instead, presents ethical norms as developing in the practical, heuristic environment of time-limited, language-equipped agents attempting to second-guess the actions and intentions of their social conspecifics. The result is a self that is extended in time and space: It can commit itself to long-term projects and can incorporate the good of others into its own selfishness. Nevertheless, what he offers is an account of the origin not just of prudential strategies for individual or species survival, but of truly ethical norms that respect the human rights and dignity of others. Ultimately, what we want from ethics is not just a norm for distinguishing right from wrong action, but an account of the value of human life. Unlike some sociobiological positions, Dennett's memetic theory explains how humanistic values can transcend the value of biological survival.

> My aim . . . has been to demonstrate that if we accept Darwin's "strange inversion of reasoning" we can build all the way up to the best and deepest human thought on questions of morality and

meaning, ethics and freedom. Far from being an enemy of these traditional explorations, the evolutionary perspective is an indispensable ally. I have not sought to replace the voluminous work in ethics with some Darwinian *alternative*, but rather to place that work on the foundation it deserves: a realistic, naturalistic, potentially unified vision of our place in nature. Recognizing our uniqueness as reflective, communicating animals does not require any human "exceptionalism" that must shake a defiant fist at Darwin and shun the insights to be harvested from the beautifully articulated and empirically anchored system of thought. (FE 307–308)

RELIGION

For many, the best bulwark to protect our unique humanistic values against desacralization by science is religion. But, like ethics, understanding religion is no easy task. What exactly *is* religion? How did it originate? What is its function? Is it good or is it bad? What is the future of religion? Will it wither away as science penetrates our secular society? Will it regain ground as Enlightenment rationality evaporates? Will it transform itself into creedless associations concerned with self-help, social justice, or environmental stewardship? What attitude or policy should we take to it?

In typical fashion, Dennett proposes that we answer these questions not by metaphysical arguments about the existence of God but by studying religion as a natural phenomenon. To do so, we need to define first the object "religion" that we wish to study; second, we need to discuss how evolutionary and memetic theories can be applied to religion, especially in the face of objections that they cannot, or even should not, be applied in this case; and third, we need to evaluate religion in order to discuss what our future policies toward it should be.

Study of religion

Dennett offers us a preliminary definition of religions as *"social systems whose participants avow belief in a supernatural agent or agents whose approval is to be sought"* (BS 9). The definition is intended to exclude from consideration social institutions such as Santa Claus, which we do not believe in. It also excludes private "spirituality," that is, the case of individuals whose beliefs in the supernatural do not form part of a social system; they are spiritual but not religious. Dennett also excludes "satanic cults" on the grounds that they are unholy alliances with demons and so unworthy of being counted as religious: religious people are well intentioned and wish to lead good lives. Notice that avowing belief is sufficient for inclusion; whether participants in religion actually believe in its dogmas is a different and more complex matter, as we will see.

What is essential for religion is the belief in a supernatural agent who is in certain fundamental ways similar to a human agent. Religious people pray to God (or gods), ask God for mercy and forgiveness, and offer thanks and praise. They assume God will listen, understand, and act as a result. Of course, God does not have to have a grey beard and need not be male or female, but a minimal level of anthropomorphism is crucial for the conception to count as religious. Sophisticated theologians, who believe in a God that is the eternal and immutable foundation of all being, have a conception which implies that it makes no sense for God to listen to prayer or to choose to act one way rather than another. Such believers do not count as religious under Dennett's definition. If they nonetheless participate in rituals or public prayer services in which they "avow" anthropomorphic beliefs—perhaps as metaphorical symbols—then they qualify as "religious" on these grounds.

Dennett holds that religion defined in this way is a natural behavior analogous to language, music, reproductive activities, hunting, and so on. We can, and should, investigate the genetic and psychological factors, economic and sociological elements, the historical components, and, above all, the evolutionary processes that allow us to understand it. One might well object, "is this not what historians, sociologists, anthropologists and, above all, academics in the field called 'religious studies' have been doing for centuries?" Dennett responds that these fields have tended to treat religion as a human phenomenon defined by meaning toward which one must adopt a first-person or subjective perspective. His naturalistic proposal is to reject this special methodological status and insist that religion can be studied by the standard approaches of the natural and biological sciences.

To understand the distinction, imagine we were to investigate why people fear heights. On the one hand we could study their subjective feelings or the reasons—often good ones, as it happens!—for their fear. Yet we could also study the neurophysiological mechanism of the fear or the evolutionary basis for the instinctive reaction. The second approach treats it as a "natural" phenomenon. In the same way, just because religion is a subjective experience does not mean it is exempt from objective investigation.

That the investigation should be objective does not mean that religion should only be studied by people unfamiliar with it. It is essential that those who investigate religion have a thorough grasp of the phenomenon. In recent decades there have been some infamous social studies of science by people who had only the flimsiest acquaintance with real science. This has been, in Dennett's opinion, a fiasco that must not be repeated in the case of religion. A superficial, dismissive study by unsympathetic outsiders ignorant of the profound experiences of religious people and of the social significance of religious institutions would betray the high ideals of science. On the other hand, it is equally implausible to suggest that only those who are religious can study religion. This is no more likely than the claim by some feminists that only women can study women. What is needed is neither superficial dismissal by the ill-informed nor self-serving smokescreens by insiders but the impartial application of objective natural scientific method in its full rigour.

There is an obstacle, however. In the case of religion, we are under a spell, a spell that prevents us studying religion objectively. Some believe that religion, whether true or false, has benefits that accrue only while religion is accepted uncritically. The sense that some religious people have that the objective study of religion would be blasphemous is one expression of this worry. Dennett responds, "We mustn't make the mistake of the man in the old joke who complained that, just when he'd finally succeeded in training his donkey not to eat, the stupid animal up and died on him" (BS 43–44). Consider an analogy with music: music so obviously enhances human life that, if there were reasons to believe that studying why this is so would undermine its value, we might well want to think twice before going ahead. Nevertheless, the obviously self-serving nature of this worry in the case of religion means that we cannot simply assume that it is justified. We must break the spell against investigation and, at the very least, examine whether the investigation would itself actually be damaging. Is even this risky?

On the face of it the risks seem rather low. The study of music has not reduced its aesthetic value. Despite the intense social taboo against it, the scientific study of sexuality has not undermined its importance for us; indeed the therapeutic spinoffs have enhanced the sexual life of many. Despite vehement historical opposition to the dissection of human cadavers on the grounds that it would violate the dignity of the human body, our bodies, and their dignity, have only benefited from the knowledge we have gained. The objective study of religion is needed to determine whether it is good or bad for us; a study like this might also allow us to distinguish between noxious forms of the phenomenon and religious practices that are beneficial to participants and to society.

Evolution of religion

If we took the risk and investigated religion scientifically, what might we find? To open our horizons, Dennett sketches briefly a wide range of possibilities.

Good Tricks
Some genetic or cultural features have such obvious objective advantages that they are invented and reinvented independently time and again—Good Tricks, as Dennett calls them. Money is a fine example: it is a cultural feature that so enhances exchange that it has appeared independently in many areas of the world. Some feature of religion, e.g., its capacity to create social cohesion, may make religion such a Good Trick that it has appeared in almost every culture.

Sweet tooth
But religion might turn out to be like our sweet tooth. When our ancestors were evolving, food and calories were scarce, so a taste for sweet foods gave them some evolutionary advantage. Nowadays, in those parts of the world where food is overabundant, this trait leads to obesity and ill health. It is possible that religion in the past contributed to our survival but may be noxious under current circumstances. It had a (free-floating) rationale that has now lapsed.

Cultural/genetic side-effects
Some phenomena have appeared as genetic side-effects of technological or other cultural developments. Lactose tolerance, for example, appears only in those cultures that have domesticated

dairy animals. Religion might be a cultural/genetic side-effect like this.

Sexual selection

Perhaps religion developed as a side-effect of the sexual selection process, like the beautiful and elaborate tail of the male peacock. Another example is the male bowerbird, who builds an extraordinarily elaborate bower to impress the female; because the female bowerbird selects her mate on the basis of these bowers, natural selection has resulted in male birds obsessed with the building of bowers. Archaeological evidence from the Palaeolithic period reveals a surprisingly large number of highly elaborated stone axes, so elaborate as to be nonfunctional. Some have suggested that these had a role similar to that of peacock tails: they demonstrated the high competence of some individuals to their potential mates who therefore had a reproductive advantage. It is possible that in some human cultures, a sexual selection process like this led to the development of music as females chose to mate with those who could sing the sweetest. Could a similar process explain religion? Males who possessed religious traits might have been particularly appealing to females. The result could have been selection pressure for the development of religion.

Opiate of the masses

Alternatively, religion might function like an addiction. Some brain mechanisms were designed to maintain appropriate levels of dopamine but these mechanisms can be hijacked by cocaine, nicotine, heroin, and so on, producing an addiction to these drugs. It is possible that religion hijacked some genetic or cultural system designed originally for a different purpose.

Pearl theory

It is possible that religion is like a pearl: some minor irritant that results in a highly elaborate—and valuable—structure as a reaction.

Many of the above

Dennett himself is not committed to any of these theories; he wants to avoid speculative, single-factor theories that prematurely quieten our curiosity and undermine the only real way forward: solid scientific research. Widespread as religion is, he is unsympathetic to those who think we can discover universal, genetic human needs or characteristics that can explain the details of religious belief or practice—though ultimately this is an empirical question. A multifactorial explanation is the most likely: religion is a contingent development that depends on the historical interaction of a number of evolutionary forces acting in unison. While Dennett's primary aim is to promote the scientific investigation of religion in order to develop a well-grounded theory based on evidence, he is willing to offer a tentative account of the nature of religion as an example of what a well-developed theory might look like. The account is consonant with his previous treatment of consciousness, ethics, selfhood, and so on. We will look at two likely stages of evolution sketched out by Dennett: first, the prereligious, basic contributing factors, and then the development of organized, institutional religion.

There was a time in our evolutionary history when there were no religions; now there are many. While there are a few dozen major religions with millions of believers, there are thousands of smaller ones. Two or three religions come into existence every day, but typically they last less than a decade. Over the span of human history religions may number in the millions. While the first archaeological evidence of religion dates to about 25,000 years ago, it is likely that religious practices and beliefs originated well before that date.

The most promising place to start is with the recognition of agents. Organisms of any species must be able to recognize their conspecifics, but human sociality requires the ability to recognize other humans as agents, that is, entities with beliefs and desires to whom the intentional stance may be applied. Attributing beliefs and desires to animals is a natural, and useful, extension of this capacity. When the ability is extended to plants or inanimate objects—call it a *hyperactive agent detection device* (HADD)—then we have anthropomorphism, or animism. Since animism may sometimes lead to useful predictions, groups who adopt it may have an evolutionary advantage. Believing that the spirit of the seals leads them to present themselves for killing on ice floes at the same place and time each year is a very successful meme. Continuing to apply intentional categories to ancestors after their death is a similar extension. HADD, then, may be one of the first, gradual steps toward religion.

Another step is likely to be divination. Decision-making, especially by groups, may be hampered by underconfidence. Circumstances may require a decision even though many factors may still be unknown. A shaman who performs a ritual—examining the entrails of an animal perhaps—may give a group confidence to proceed with its best, though uncertain option. The procedure also lets leaders off the hook if things go wrong. Divination is a meme that may well give a group a survival advantage.

Another contributing factor is ritual. In the evolutionary context, information transmitted from generation to generation needs to be protected to ensure its fidelity. This is as true for memes as it is for genes. Rituals may be self-protective techniques for memes. The figures of a ritual, a religious dance for example, are held in the memory of many different people so that when the dance is actually performed the majority can correct any faults in the memory of an individual. Formulas or dogmas may be memorized by rote and they are often couched in ways participants do not understand; as a result, they get passed on verbatim without the modifications that are likely to occur if individuals passed on the gist of what they understood.

Appealing to ancestors is likely to have an even more important survival benefit. In social interactions, knowing what strategic information others have access to is often very important. Does anyone know that I stole that pig? The fantasy of a "full-access agent" who, knowing other people's desires and intentions, could advise me unerringly is a powerful idea. Given my childhood experience of my parents' superiority with such skills, it is understandable that I would project this capacity onto my ancestors. Imagining what my parents would do in my tricky situation may in fact often be useful, but developing confidence in this imagining is a problem. Rituals and shamanistic ceremonies that reveal what gods or oracles have to say may well make this easier and so facilitate social relations.

These kinds of factors cluster into basic proto-religion. *Folk religion*, as Dennett calls it, is characterized by the absence of self-consciousness: the rituals and beliefs are not reflected upon or recognized for what they are. In the next stage, as he sees it, folk religion spawns organized religion in a way analogous to the way folk music gives rise to professional musicians, scores, concert halls, and critics.

Consider the meme of healing the sick—often carried out by shamans in folk religion. Using procedures akin to hypnotism—similar to the placebo-effect—shamans may actually improve the health of individuals and groups, if only by giving people hope. As practitioners become more aware of their own techniques, they may discuss them with other shamans and start to teach them to apprentices in a more or less systematic manner. Such discussion may encourage the representation of rationales that were originally free-floating. If trance is associated with healing, it may, traditionally and without reflection, have been achieved by dancing. Discussing it with others may lead practitioners to think explicitly of trance as the reason for the dancing. The previously free-floating rationale thereby passes over into a represented rationale.

Religion then becomes a craft with professionals who master and hand on the tricks of the trade, often to an elite and secret group, a guild. Many of the memes involved in religion come to be examined and methods are actively devised to promote them. The simple self-perpetuation of folk religion is replaced by conscious design. Religion moves beyond superstition and becomes domesticated. Stewards appear who recognize that religion must be fostered and handed down consciously from generation to generation. The result is a loose guild, an organization with some internal structure and with secret knowledge, that, while initially dedicated to healing, later develops an interest in the preservation of the guild for its own sake. The importance of preserving the guild itself then becomes a new value over and beyond the value of healing. The result is the passage from folk religion to institutionalized religion, to religion as a structure or organization promoted by stewards dedicated to the task.

Institutional religion

Like genes, memes that replicate successfully usually rely on self-protective mechanisms to ensure their faithful reproduction. The doubling of the DNA helix is an example of a protective mechanism for genes. Dennett proposes that the persistence of institutional religions is partly due to one particularly effective technique of self-protection: the use of second-order beliefs.

Many social institutions, besides religion, rely for their preservation on second-order beliefs about the institution. Scientific method is a case in point: it is protected by the second-order belief that science is a good thing. Therefore funding should be provided and students should be recruited into scientific careers. Similarly the meme for democracy comes with the second-order belief that democracy is the most valid mode of governance and hence citizens should be actively encouraged to support democracy. In the case of religion, it is often believed that it is impolite to doubt or challenge another's beliefs or even to publicly express doubts about one's own. Some religions consider doubt to be diabolical, temptations inspired by the devil, so doubters are to be shunned and even the entertaining of one's own doubts must be rejected as sinful. The most important self-protective mechanism, however, is the belief in belief.

The second-order belief that belief in religion is a good thing is particularly prominent in rationalist societies, that is, in the face of the questioning of religion. It is particularly visible in the case of people who, though they have no religious beliefs themselves, still think that it is important for society, or for individuals, that the idea of religious belief be promoted. Some parents who are themselves no longer religious, nevertheless consider it their duty to introduce their children to religious practices because these are in one way or another good for them. Politicians may think that promoting religious belief improves the moral caliber of citizens even though they themselves may be above such things. This belief in belief results in atheists, doubters, and believers all cooperating to protect, preserve, and replicate the memes of religion.

The belief in belief also serves to obscure a fundamental difference between anthropomorphic fundamentalists and more theologically sophisticated thinkers. While Dennett includes, as part of his definition of religion, the idea of a personal God who can perform actions in the world and listen to prayer, he realizes that there are more sophisticated "believers" who conceptualize God as some impersonal spiritual force in the universe, as the Totality of All Things, as the Ground of Being, and so on. (If the term "God" is used to designate the totality of the world—as perhaps Spinoza does—then atheism is a logical impossibility.) In principle such thinkers are on a quite different wavelength than those who accepted an anthropomorphic God, but the protective, second-order belief in belief obscures this conflict. After all, both camps believe that they have religious beliefs; they both believe that they believe in God. That the contents of their beliefs might be diametrically opposed is obscured by a superficial resemblance: they both accept that "belief in God" is a good thing. While this purely verbal similarity reduces conflict, it also serves as an excellent self-protective mechanism for the replication of religious memes.

But is it a purely verbal similarity? An alternative interpretation is that what we have here is a case of division of doxastic labor. Many people believe that plutonium can be used to make nuclear fission bombs. The vast majority of such people, nonetheless, have very little understanding of what nuclear fission is, and would be unable to recognize plutonium if they came across any. This does not mean that they don't share the belief; it just means that ordinary people rely upon experts to define the meaning of their technical terms. I can meaningfully incorporate the term plutonium into my belief because I can rely upon experts who really know what the term means. Could it be the same in the case of religion? Is it not possible that the ordinary believer can meaningfully profess belief in God by leaving it to the theological experts to give content to that term? Children, after all, learn to recite religious formulas while leaving it to their parents to ensure that their verbalisms have a real meaning. When they become adults, they may repeat religious rituals while relying on their shaman or priest to do the understanding for them.

Yet could it be that their religious minister has no more grasp of the content than they do, but has simply received the formulas from her mentors?

Many an anthropologist of religion has faced the problem that, while she can record what her informants say they believe, she has trouble grasping what these professions of faith really mean in the mind of the informant. Dennett thinks that the informants themselves may be in a similar predicament: they know what to say, but assume someone else in their community knows what it means. It is therefore possible that even if nobody does, the formulas may well be passed on from generation to generation without anyone realizing this fact. In other words, what we may have in the case of religion is a society of people *professing* their beliefs without anyone actually *having* such beliefs. Indeed if one takes Wittgenstein's arguments about private language seriously, the belief is the professing. Not only is there no way for the anthropologist to know what her informant really believes; there is no way for an individual to know himself what he does or does not believe. Nevertheless, the second-order belief in belief facilitates the replication of the profession of faith whether the beliefs have a content or not.

Ultimately the issue reduces to the problem of radical translation. Two adherents of the same religion may profess the same formula while the content of their beliefs may be quite different. There may even be no content to their beliefs. Wittgenstein's argument depends on the possibility that while one person is referring to a beetle in their box, another person may be using the same terms for a rock in their box. The box might even be empty. Whether others give the same meanings as I do to their words can only be determined by pragmatic interaction and coherence and so I can never have absolute certainty about my translation of their language. The peculiar nature of religious language exacerbates this problem. Hence, according to Dennett, the attribution of belief refers, in effect, only to the external profession of faith: that is what counts for an adherent's membership in the community. Extremely paradoxical beliefs—this is both wine and blood—may serve to bring out the crucial importance of professing over believing since the paradoxical nature of the belief emphasizes the point that the participant does not understand what she is saying. Her act of faith is her professing it nonetheless. Her inability to understand the paradox also emphasizes her sense of dependence upon others in the community—the experts are the only authorities. Her identity as a member of the community is thereby reinforced.

The problem is particularly acute in the case of beliefs not directly linked to action. It is because most everyday beliefs influence how people act that we usually have little trouble grasping what others believe. Many religious beliefs—the Christian Trinity, transubstantiation, etc.—have no obvious implications for behavior other than the verbal or ritual act of professing. Such beliefs are often declared to be "mysteries," that is, their content cannot be understood by anyone. In such cases all we are left with are the acts of professing. Dennett therefore suggests that the external professing of belief is more central in religion than the content of the belief itself.

The central point is that, in any evolutionary process, inherited information needs protective mechanisms if it is to be transmitted faithfully. Although he mentions a number of self-protective mechanisms for institutionalized religion, Dennett thinks that the belief in belief is among the most central.

Evaluation of religion

Given the techniques of self-protection, it is not surprising that it is difficult to evaluate objectively whether religion is good or bad.

There is a danger of irrational presumptions: believers may assume that religion is good for us; some nonbelievers may assume it is bad. Only a scientific study of the issue can determine the question one way or the other.

There is one simplistic evaluation that should be avoided. Just granting that an evolutionary account can be given does not automatically mean that religion is good. Memes need to be evaluated much like parasites or foreign bacteria that, as part of their survival techniques, have come to live within our bodies: some may be toxic for us; some—mutualists—may improve the survival chances of the host; and others may be neutral. The parasite *Toxoplasma gondii* makes rats that it infects foolhardy so that they are easily caught by cats who thereby ingest the parasite. The process promotes the life cycle of the parasite, but is hardly beneficial for the rats. We cannot simply assume that, since the human species and religion have survived together, religion is good for humans.

How could we evaluate whether religion is good? First, we might ask whether it improves our physical or mental health. It is relatively easy to see how such questions might be objectively investigated. For example, some researchers have studied whether people who are ill heal faster if others pray for them. Ironically, if patients are told that they are being prayed for, they actually do worse than average—possibly because they assume they must be very ill if people are praying for them.

A second, more difficult question is whether religion makes us morally good. There are many examples of religious people doing good—the abolition of slavery; caring for the sick—but it is just as easy to point to evils committed in the name of religion—the Crusades; the Inquisition; religiously motivated terrorism. The suggestion that religion motivates people to do good in order to achieve an eternal reward or to avoid evil out of fear of divine retribution offers a demeaning view of human nature, in Dennett's opinion: truly moral people act out of respect for others or for the good to be achieved. Maybe religion makes us good by offering the gods as role models for good behavior; unfortunately, in many religions the gods model immoral behavior—think of Greek, or Maori gods. It might be claimed that religions give us rules of conduct that make us more moral. However, religious rules of conduct, e.g., the Judaic/Christian/Islamic biblical injunction that homosexuals are to be executed, cannot simply be taken on face value as moral: they must be submitted to public reason. Which religious rules are to be taken literally and which ones should be rejected must be decided on the basis of moral norms external to each religion.

On the other hand, we cannot assume that nonreligious people are immoral. It is sometimes suggested that, since many nonbelievers are materialists, they must therefore lack a sense of morality. But this is a confusion of terms. If "materialist" refers to a consumerist lifestyle then it is far from clear that, in contemporary society, the religious are in practice more virtuous than atheists. If "materialist" refers to a philosophical position that opposes a metaphysical dualism of matter and spirit then there is no obvious link between materialism and a lack of morality. Materialists in the metaphysical sense are no more likely to be materialists in the consumerist sense than are dualists.

But what about spirituality? Are "spiritual" people not more moral? The term is hard to pin down. Sometimes spiritual people are represented as those who appreciate the wonders of nature, a peaceful and meditative life, or the value of aesthetic experience. Apart from the fact that nonbelievers may share these characteristics, such spirituality may give rise to an obsession with one's own inner life to the detriment of one's obligations to act morally in the wider world by fighting injustice or promoting peace.

Whether religion makes us morally good, is, then, still an open question. We should avoid making rash assumptions and submit the question to objective investigation.

Finally, what could one say of the argument that religion is good because it gives meaning to life? Dennett considers the case of "fraudulent" religions, that is, sects consciously created by tricksters to make money from the gullible. When the fraud is successful, members of the congregation become fervent practitioners, find new meaning in their lives, and may even overcome addiction or other life problems. If this is true in the case of fraudulent religions, then it might well be that, in the case of sincere religions, participants lead richer lives even if the religious dogmas they believe in are objectively false.

In any case, Dennett's speculations about the effects of religion on health, moral conduct, spirituality, or a meaningful life aim to lay out the questions. The answers, he insists, must come from objective, empirical research.

What to do?

In the meantime, while awaiting the results of the research, is there anything we should be *doing* about religion? Dennett offers a couple of pieces of advice.

First, we should encourage tolerance. In many contemporary societies there is a peculiar ambivalence toward religions other than one's own: although officially many faiths maintain the dogma that only their own adherents are saved and those outside their own sect are damned, in practice the general social belief in the value of any religious belief—the belief in belief—leads to an everyday tolerance of other religions. This amounts to treating others' gods much as we treat Santa Claus: the important issue is how the belief improves people's lives rather than whether the belief is true or false. Dennett suggests, or maybe hopes, that religious communities will develop the attitude we have toward sports teams: while we may passionately insist that the team we identify with is the best, on a rational level we realize that there is nothing absolute involved and that others have as much right to support their team as we do. The only important thing is that we support some team or other. On the other hand, since he also believes in the value of truth, he worries that a society in which people get their life's meaning from false beliefs would be a society of hypocrites.

True or false, people have a right to their beliefs. If individuals want to isolate themselves from rational discussion or the results of scientific investigation, they should be allowed to do so. Communal rights, on the other hand, are more problematic. Does the community, religious or otherwise, have the right to insulate its members from ideas the community leaders disagree with? In the Indian Ocean the inhabitants of the Andaman and Nicobar Islands have refused all contact with the modern world in order to maintain their Stone Age culture. Is this a matter of the leaders keeping the majority in ignorance? Whatever we think about the adults, the children are being indoctrinated into an attitude that will prevent them from accessing the information about the modern world that they would need to be able to make a rational decision for themselves.

Yet do not all parents have the right to control their children's ideas? Dennett is very doubtful about this principle. We accept that society should intervene in the case of physical abuse of children, even by their parents. Many think that children of alcoholics or of smokers are at risk and that it may be ethical to intervene. In the case of religious cults, it seems clear that early indoctrination of children may enclose them in ideological prisons they would have great difficulty escaping from even when adults. Just as we should avoid the racial stereotyping of children, should we not also avoid stereotyping them as Leninist children, conservative children, or Catholic children? While parents clearly have the first responsibility for the upbringing of their children and the right to transmit their values to them—this is the essence of "family values"—this right must be limited by the need to assure the future freedom of the child when it becomes independent. If parents attempt to isolate their children from alternative ideas, whether at home or in insulating schools, then we should see this as abuse. Schools, like the mass media, must not be simply propaganda tools: they must promote a rational discussion of religion on the basis of scientific and objective evidence.

We also cannot wait for the results of scientific investigation to deal with "toxic" religions. Even those who defend the claim that religious belief is, in general, a good thing, realize that there are some cults that, either because of the desire for profit or because of the mental instability of their leaders, are noxious for their vulnerable adherents and for society. Their propaganda amounts to false advertising: some means must be found to control such institutions and those parts of the mass media that promote them.

Fundamentally, claims Dennett, religion must be subject to public debate based on reason and evidence. Institutions that do not support this principle have no place in our society: democracy must trump faith.

*   *   *

Dennett's ideas about the nature and origin of ethics and religion rely on the same conceptual tools with which he approaches consciousness, selfhood and freedom: evolutionary gradualism, memetic replication, and so on. Yet, in the case of religion, there is a notable change of attitude. While he enthusiastically defends freedom against those who think it is an illusion, he seems deeply suspicious of religion. While he admires selfhood as a magnificent creation that humanity should be immensely proud of, God and gods, though they are constructed memetically in a parallel manner, are treated as irredeemably illusory. Absolutist foundations for ethics are rejected, but Dennett's heuristic account of the origin of morality clearly endorses, even if it does not technically justify, ethical values. Indeed, Dennett himself expresses strong support for human rights. He doesn't suggest that we need further objective research into whether ethics is a good thing—or consciousness, freedom or selfhood, for that matter. He simply assumes that they should be included in "the things we hold dear." His heuristic account of religion, in sharp contrast, does not culminate in any wholehearted approval of what has been created. Some religions are positively "toxic," but even those that aren't are, he hints, beyond their shelf-life. I find no clear basis in his theoretical analysis of memetic constructs for this disparity between the endorsement of ethics and the ambivalence toward religion. He may, of course, have other—political or personal—reasons.

In his defence, Dennett might argue that his system does not automatically endorse every evolutionary or memetic development. Not all memes are good for their hosts. An evolutionary account of the origin of war would not necessarily lead us to admire it! And to give him his due, Dennett never in fact dismisses religion outright. "The only prescription I will make categorically and without reservation," he says, is "do more research" (BS 311).

CHAPTER 9

CONCLUSION: SYNTHESIS AND CRITICAL ASSESSMENT

Dennett's philosophy is a synthesis of contemporary thought, a global worldview. While his focus is on the nature of consciousness, of mind, and of selfhood, his account of these issues requires him to integrate them into a theory about the place of meaning, value, and human dignity within the natural world. In this concluding chapter, I will pick out a number of the central themes in Dennett's philosophy that recur throughout his works and that integrate his thought into one unified philosophy: opposition to metaphysics; stances and levels of reality; the Darwinian algorithm; gradualism; and, crucially, language.

CENTRAL THEMES

First, a rejection of metaphysics runs throughout Dennett's work. Philosophers have traditionally searched for an absolute viewpoint, an Archimedean stand beyond the relativistic world of body, language, history and situation—what Dennett calls the "God's eye view." A God, outside space and time, could know how things really are. Dennett repudiates this appeal to an absolute standpoint and the notion of reality-in-itself that comes with it. Instead, he wants to humanize knowledge, to deal with everyday reality, and to rely upon the best view of the world that current science can deliver. His is a continuation of the Kantian project: knowledge is limited to the phenomenal world, to things as we experience them, and to what can be verified.

It is the God's eye view that misleads qualophiles into thinking of qualia as realities that are what they are regardless of how we experience them. Likewise, it is only from the God's eye view that one could conceive of reality as independent of stances. The idea of the self as a spiritual substance beyond the physical world and free of determinism is modelled on this kind of transcendent God.

Instead, following Quine and Ryle as much as Kant, Dennett adopts a pragmatic, heuristic, and everyday approach to the world. Accepting the phenomenal world we experience, and the empirical world revealed by natural science, is not incompatible with the human values we hold so dear: selfhood, dignity, freedom, and ethics. Rather than denigrating such values by reducing them to the physical, Dennett holds that materialism can offer them a more solid foundation than absolutist metaphysics ever could.

Secondly, Dennett replaces the traditional God's eye approach with his theory of stances. The physical, design, and intentional stances—and there could conceivably be others—are pragmatic, strategic viewpoints accessible to organisms immersed in space and time, and struggling for survival. Each stance reveals objects, not things that are beings-in-themselves, but realities that depend upon the context of the stance for being the kinds of things that they are. Thus, realities come in different levels that, although they are related, cannot be greedily reduced to one another. Selfhood and consciousness are revealed as realities from the intentional stance; they are related to physical and functional realities, but are not reducible to them.

A third recurring theme in Dennett's work is Darwin's evolutionary paradigm. Dennett maintains that we must be able to get here from there: what whatever we are discussing—consciousness, self, freedom, ethics—there was a time when they did not exist and so there must be an account of their coming to be. The framework for any such account is the adaptationist algorithm: the survival of the fittest. While Dennett often speaks of memetic analysis as if this were a unique approach, his central insight is that the Darwinian algorithm is abstract: its logical structure is independent of the medium that it operates in, so it applies indifferently to cultural, biological, and even computational processes. Memes can be explained by the same principles that allow us to explain genes: the memes that are best adapted to their (cultural) environment survive. Hence there is no methodological dichotomy between the natural and cultural (or human) sciences: one unified mode of understanding covers biology, culture, and language.

Dennett's antiessentialism follows from this evolutionary approach. Since Aristotle, we have thought of biological organisms as differentiated into distinct species, with each species being defined by its own intrinsic essence. The Darwinian method requires us to reject such discrete, essential distinctions. Evolution advances by small, gradual steps. Over time, there is a continuum of gradually evolving organisms, and the apparent rigid distinction between species is an artefact of the narrow time-slice in which we observe them. Appeal to intrinsic essences has no place in this scheme.

But it is not only in biology that essences must be repudiated: Dennett opposes essentialist thinking throughout his philosophy. The notion of a quale as a distinct, intrinsically defined element of consciousness is the result of essentialist thinking. Instead Dennett offers a contextualist account: conscious states are defined by their relationships to other states, to action, and to language, and to their future fame in the brain. The essentialist understanding of selfhood is likewise rejected in favor of the memetic and social construction of a form of organization capable of accepting responsibility. Selves appear gradually in evolution as in childhood; they may be multiple or partial; and their scope can extend and contract. Similarly, freedom comes in degrees: acts may be more or less free, rather than the rigid dichotomy between free and unfree acts that essentialist thinking requires. Just as there is no first mammal, there is no first free act or conscious state: in principle, there are always intermediate phenomena whose status cannot be neatly defined by cut and dried categories.

This is also true of language, perhaps the most central theme in Dennett's work. There is no rigid boundary between semantic (or meaningful) and causal processes. In the brain, neural processes inherit semantic properties from their larger context. The result is not only public language, but consciousness, for the interpretation of language is the basis of heterophenomenology, which, in the end, is our only access to consciousness. Not only for others, but for ourselves, what we sincerely say we are aware of defines our consciousness. Language is also the most significant medium for the transmission of memes. The social interactions with others that give rise to selves are above all mediated by language. A free act is one that we can be asked, in language, to perform—or can ask ourselves to perform. Language permeates the whole of Dennett's philosophy, especially his account of the human world.

These themes unite Dennett's philosophy into a coherent whole. He does not, of course, claim to be the originator of these ideas. On the contrary, he is generous in his acknowledgment of the sources for his philosophical inspiration. He owes much to Quine: Dennett's account of the attribution of belief, he points out, is indebted to Quine's discussion of radical interpretation. Ryle's opposition to metaphysical dualism and his interpretation of mental concepts in terms of everyday language and dispositions is at the heart of Dennett's rejection of mental representations. The idea that the author of a heterophenomenological account cannot be wrong about how things seem to her parallels Husserl's phenomenological reduction and may originate from what Dennett calls a "deeply influential dose of Husserl from Dagfinn Follesdal" (DP 362). That there are different modes of reality, each relative to a stance, is strikingly similar to Husserl's position that there are different realms of being, each constituted by transcendental intersubjectivity; so this concept too may be an effect of the same dose. The dependence of entities on their context is a theme already found in Wittgenstein's theory of language games. The narrative nature of selfhood is a common theme in postmodernism. The centrality of language has been a central preoccupation throughout the 20th century in both the phenomenological and analytic traditions. What distinguishes Dennett's philosophy is his synthesis of these many streams of thought—and many others—with the concrete results of investigations by the natural sciences and his creation of an overall philosophy within which they can all fit coherently together.

In this synthesis, philosophy must work closely with science. One of its most important roles is to undermine the bugbears that impede the scientific study of human phenomena. (The subtitle of one of his books, *Sweet Dreams*, is "Philosophical Obstacles to a Science of Consciousness.") Absolutist preconceptions about the nature of consciousness, freedom, and ethics have often prevented us from taking advantage of the insights we can derive from the scientific investigation of these issues. A more pragmatic and naturalistic philosophy is more likely to yield a unified worldview. As he puts it:

> My fundamental perspective is *naturalism*, the idea that philosophical investigations are not superior to, or prior to, investigations in the natural sciences, but in partnership with those

truth-seeking enterprises, and that the proper job for philosophers here is to clarify and unify the often warring perspectives into a single vision of the universe. That means welcoming the bounty of well-won scientific discoveries and theories as raw material for philosophical theorizing, so that informed, constructive criticism of both science and philosophy is possible. (FE 14–15)

CRITICAL ASSESSMENT

The synthesis that Dennett attempts is an ambitious one. Does it succeed? The answer is controversial and has led to a large literature of criticism in books and journals. (A sampling of critical books about Dennett's philosophy can be found in the bibliography.) We have already seen, in previous chapters, how Dennett has responded in a dialogical fashion to specific arguments against his positions, using the objections to clarify his own stand. It is one thing, however, to respond to criticisms of particular positions; it is another to evaluate Dennett's system as a whole. As an introduction, this book is aimed primarily at exposition of Dennett's thought, so an overall assessment of the success of his synthesis is beyond its scope. Nevertheless, it is worth sketching out very briefly some of the threats his system faces and some of the potential directions a critical assessment might take.

Method

First, there is the problem of Dennett's philosophical method. While he often offers arguments, a significant proportion of Dennett's writings involves analogies, metaphors, intuition pumps, and Just So stories. Is this an adequate method for justifying philosophical positions? Dennett is a brilliant writer, full of witty expressions, vibrant language, and colorful images. Is this a virtue or a vice? Is the reader simply convinced by the provocative analogies and persuasive language?

In his defence, Dennett might say that the main aim of his philosophy is to liberate us from a picture that holds us captive, to free us from imaginary bugbears, to remove conceptual obstacles, and to open up new territory for real scientists to explore. His synthesis is programmatic: he is not laying down a final dogma, but offering a new vision, a new framework for further research. The function of Dennett's many thought-experiments and illustrative scenarios is not to offer a half-baked scientific theory but to overcome a certain philosophical inability to imagine what a scientific theory of the phenomenon could look like. By offering us a sketch of a theory, he frees our imagination from its shackles and liberates science to pursue directions previously thought to be impossible. The details of the framework—the evolutionary Just So stories, the speculations about the development of language, the game theory suggestions for the foundations of ethics, the stages in the history of religion, and so on—are presented tentatively, as illustrations of the kinds of approaches his new framework would open up. The metaphorical or speculative details may get him into trouble, but rigorous arguments may not be the most appropriate way to propose a new vision. As Rorty puts it, "There is no over-arching ahistorical context-free criterion to which one can appeal when asked to shift from one paradigm of explanation to another" (DC 188).

Science

One might have expected Dennett to move beyond metaphors at least in the case of science. The new paradigm is founded on it, so is an account of the status of science not essential to his project? Traditionally, many philosophers have made the justification of science a central focus—think of Descartes, Kant, or Husserl. Of the many areas Dennett's synthesis must unify, science is surely among the most important. Yet a developed philosophy of science is absent in his philosophy. He proclaims that science is our best way of understanding the natural world, but offers little justification for this belief. His naturalism could be caricatured as follows: grant science; assume it is correct; and now show how, on this foundation, the things we hold dear can be preserved. Dennett sets out to reconcile human values to the scientific worldview; but he does little to tell us why we should adopt the scientific worldview in the first place.

The problem is particularly acute given Dennett's theory of stances. If stances are alternative strategies for finding useful order in the world, it is hard to see why one stance should have any privilege over any other. Yet Dennett speaks of the "hegemony" of the physical and design stances over the intentional (IS 109). Dennett's instinct as a materialistic naturalist inclines him to treat the natural world as relatively unproblematic. It is the intentional world that needs to be reconciled to it rather than vice versa. There is an unresolved tension between the egalitarianism of the three stances and the elitism of the scientific worldview.

The neglect of philosophy of science is especially surprising given Dennett's account of language. Science is not just ink on paper in scientific journals; it is the meaning these marks have for scientists as conscious people. Science involves texts, heterophenomenological texts that express the beliefs and theories of scientists. Presumably, scientific texts are generated by the pandemonium process that, on Dennett's account, is at the origin of all language. They must be interpreted, like all language, from the intentional stance. Scientific objects would therefore seem to have the same status as any other heterophenomenological objects. Indeed, if Dennett were to pursue this line of thought, is it not intentionality that would have to account for science rather than science accounting for intentionality? One could well ask why Dennett does not take this direction, and where it might lead him if he did.

Realism

Might it lead him into Rortyian-style pragmatism? Dennett claims that the distinction between how things appear and how they really are makes sense in the external, visual world, but that the distinction does not apply when "taken all the way in." Rorty invites Dennett to take this rejection of the real-seeming distinction within consciousness "all the way out" and abandon the distinction even in the world beyond consciousness. That is, Rorty thinks we should give up the distinction between appearance and reality, even in science. So he considers Dennett's reliance on ultimate, real patterns to be misguided. There is no difference between a real and a very useful, but only apparent, pattern (DC 196). ". . . [A]ll the reasons we have for getting rid of a captivating but trouble-making picture of the mind, 'the Cartesian Theater,' . . . are also reasons for . . . [offering] a new set of metaphors for talking about the goal of science . . .", says Rorty (DC 198). Science does not aim at revealing the reality behind appearances: it is just one other way—on a par with the intentional stance—for dealing pragmatically with the world.

Dennett resists, clinging to the reality of the patterns that underlie the success of our predictive strategies. It is hard to see, however, how Dennett is being consistent in holding out, since his theory of stances would seem to place him in the same pragmatic camp as Rorty. Since there can be no independent verification, what is added to the claim, "stances find patterns that are predictive" when Dennett says, "because the underlying patterns are real"? It is hard to see what remains of Dennett's realism—"mild" as it might be.

Interpretation

Falling away from realism into pure pragmatism is not the only danger he faces. Dennett's realism is a delicate balancing act; his view is placed firmly on a "knife-edge," and, as he says, his "critics have persistently tried to show that [his] position tumbles into one abyss or the other" (IS 37). This is true of his naturalism in general.

Take his rejection of mind-body dualism, for instance. Can he not be accused of falling into a new dualism of his own? His heterophenomenological method distinguishes what is really going on from how it seems to the reporting subject. That is, the mechanism that produces the report must be clearly distinguished from the content of it. The vehicle is not the meaning. Conan Doyle is not Sherlock Holmes. The representing process is radically different from what is represented. For Descartes, mind and body have at least this much in common: they are both substances. Is Dennett's dichotomy between reality and meaning not much more radical? Should Dennett be called a radical dualist?

Is this any harm? Is it not precisely the beauty of the heterophenomenological method that it overcomes this dichotomy so that we can have one, integrated scientific approach? Dennett makes two claims for the heterophenomenological method. On the one hand, it gives us an objective method for studying consciousness. On the other, it moves us to the semantic level, for the method attributes a meaning to the sounds made by the reporting subject; the interpretation (into English, or whatever language is being used) by the stenographers attributes a content to the report. But are these claims compatible?

The method requires the stenographers who interpret the report to agree with each other; if they fail to, then their notes are jettisoned. Does this ensure objectivity? Dennett, as we saw in Chapter 6, rejects the absolute or metaphysical understanding of objectivity given by industrial strength realists: it makes no sense to speak of the stenographers' notes corresponding with some fact of the matter, with what the stream of sounds coming from the reporter *really* means. We must settle for heuristic objectivity: the stenographers attribute a meaning to the sounds within the context of English (or whatever) and if they can replicate each other's results, we accept them. In practice, objectivity is replicability. Is this enough?

At most, what Dennett has delivered is a local objectivity. The replicability of the stenographers' notes is restricted to the context of English. Within the context of Chinese, they make no sense. It is the nature of all interpretation, of all attribution of meaning, that it is relative to its context in this way.

Heterophenomenology is therefore an interpretative science. It is curious that, in discussing religion, Dennett disparages social science methods, e.g., traditional religious studies, and contrasts them with natural scientific approaches to religion, which he is advocating. In the study of consciousness, however, he is arguing that semantic interpretation is a valid, objective, scientific method. Do these two positions cohere?

But this problem is only the tip of the iceberg. According to the theory of stances, the attribution of properties is never a simple correspondence of words and things but always involves a contextual interpretation of the situation from within the relevant stance. So our concern is no longer just with consciousness or religion; all modes of objectivity—all sciences—have an interpretative structure. In the case of religion, Dennett appears to be advocating that natural science methods replace interpretation, but could Dennett not be accused, in the end, of doing the very opposite—of assimilating all scientific methodology to interpretation? This kind of analysis of Dennett's philosophy might save him from radical dualism, but only by making him a pan-interpretationist—a new abyss for a would-be naturalist to fall into. Dennett attacks greedy reductionism for trying to reduce the human to the physical. Pursuing the interpretationist direction, however, could well lead to him falling in the opposite direction: to reducing all science and objectivity to interpretation.

Maybe this is what Rorty is effectively urging him to do. Indeed, such a scheme of local objectivities within interpretative contexts is the hallmark of postmodernism rather than naturalism. It is therefore an unlikely turn for Dennett's philosophy to take. Can he, in the end, avoid it? Is he not doomed to be a postmodernist?

"Postmodernism" is so ill-defined that there is little hope for a definitive answer, but it is worth noting that the centrality of language in postmodernism is echoed in the central role it plays in Dennett's account of narrative selfhood, of consciousness, of freedom, and of ethics. On the other hand, while postmoderns tend to emphasize the incommensurability of disparate communities of meaning, Dennett's aim is to integrate the various stances into one worldview. Perhaps that is why he clings so adamantly to the fundamental reality of patterns: this reality is the anchor that holds the system together. Naturalism aims at one integrated system. Postmoderns tend to be suspicious of the ideal of synthesis in the first place. Lyotard, for example, rejects the notion of a Grand Narrative, of any overarching scheme of thought that could unify local "knowledges." The simple fact that Dennett even attempts to synthesize the human and natural disqualifies him from postmodernism and confirms his credentials as a naturalist.

* * *

This sketch of a few critical approaches to Dennett's thought makes no pretence to being complete. Much more could, and has, been said for and against it. In the end, it is the integrating vision that is the most exciting aspect of Dennett's philosophy and it is the destiny of this overall vision that will determine whether his philosophy as a whole is a failure or a success. He aims at a comprehensive worldview that resolves the conflict between humanistic phenomena and values, on the one hand, and the natural science tradition, on the other—a conflict that has bedevilled Western culture since the beginning of modern science. Ideally, his work could play a role analogous to the great medieval syntheses between philosophy and theology in the 13th century. Like the medieval syntheses, Dennett's system has specific issues that need further elaboration and particular criticisms that remain unanswered, but these are, in a sense, secondary. As a vision of how science can progress by integrating physical, biological, and human phenomena within the one conceptual scheme, his system is best understood as a comprehensive research project. Like any research project, the final judgement on its value is a heuristic one. Only the future can tell whether the project will prove to be fruitful.

BIBLIOGRAPHY

Dennett's homepage includes a link to his curriculum vitae.
http://ase.tufts.edu/cogstud/incbios/dennettd/dennettd.htm
A complete, and continuously updated, bibliography of Dennett's writings can be found at http://ase.tufts.edu/cogstud/incbios/dennettd/dennettdbiblio.htm
A list of Dennett's articles, talks, and lectures (often with live links) can be found at http://ase.tufts.edu/cogstud/incpages/publctns.shtml

WORKS BY DENNETT MENTIONED IN THE TEXT

Dennett, Daniel C. (1969), *Content and Consciousness.* International Library of Philosophy and Scientific Method. New York: Humanities Press; London: Routledge & Kegan Paul. [Coded in the text as CC]

Dennett, Daniel C. (1984), *Elbow Room: The Varieties of Free Will Worth Wanting.* Cambridge, MA: MIT Press. [Coded in the text as ER]

Dennett, Daniel C. (1986), "The self as a center of narrative gravity." http://ase.tufts.edu/cogstud/papers/selfctr.htm Consulted 07–07–2008. No pagination. [Coded in the text as CNG]

Dennett, Daniel C. (1987), *The Intentional Stance.* Cambridge, MA: MIT Press. [Coded in the text as IS]

Dennett, Daniel C. (1988), "Quining Qualia." http://ase.tufts.edu/cogstud/papers/quinqual.htm Consulted 08–01–2008. No pagination. [Coded in the text as QQ]

Dennett, Daniel C. (1991), *Consciousness Explained.* Boston: Little, Brown. [Coded in the text as CE]

Dennett, Daniel C. (1995), *Darwin's Dangerous Idea: Evolution and the Meanings of Life.* New York: Simon and Schuster; London: Allen Lane. [Coded in the text as DDI]

Dennett, Daniel C. (1997), "The evolution of evaluators." http://ase.tufts.edu/cogstud/papers/siena.htm Consulted 07–07–2008. [Coded in the text as EE]

Dennett, Daniel C. (1998), *Brainchildren: Essays on Designing Minds.* Cambridge, MA: MIT Press, A Bradford Book. [Coded in the text as BC]

Dennett, Daniel C. (2000), "With a little help from my friends," in Don Ross, Andrew Brook, and David Thompson (2000), *Dennett's Philosophy: A Comprehensive Assessment.* Cambridge, MA: MIT Press. [Coded in the text as DP]

Dennett, Daniel C. (2003), *Freedom Evolves.* New York: Viking Penguin. [Coded in the text as FE]

Dennett, Daniel C. (2005), *Sweet Dreams.* Cambridge, MA: MIT Press. [Coded in the text as SD]

Dennett, Daniel C. (2006), *Breaking the Spell.* New York, NY: Viking Penguin. [Coded in the text as BS]

Dennett, Daniel C. (2008), "How to protect human dignity from science." http://www.bioethics.gov/reports/human_dignity/chapter3.html Consulted 09–01–2008. No pagination. [Coded in the text as PHD]

A SELECTION OF BOOKS IN ENGLISH ABOUT
DENNETT'S PHILOSOPHY

Brook, Andrew and Ross, Don, eds. (2002), *Daniel Dennett.* New York, NY.: Cambridge University Press.

Dahlbom, Bo, ed. (1993), *Dennett and His Critics.* Oxford: Blackwell. [Coded in the text as DC]

Edward, Minar, ed. (1994), "The Philosophy of Daniel Dennett", *Philosophical Topics*, 22: #1 and 2.

Elton, Matthew (2003), *Daniel Dennett: Reconciling Science and our Self-Conception.* Cambridge: Polity.

McCarthy, Joan (2007), *Dennett and Ricoeur on the Narrative Self.* New York, NY.: Prometheus Books.

Ross, Don, Brook, Andrew, and Thompson, David (2000), *Dennett's Philosophy: A Comprehensive Assessment.* Cambridge, MA: MIT Press.

Roy, Jean-Michel et al. (2007), *Phenomenology and the Cognitive Sciences*, 6: # 1 and 2.

Symons, John (2002), *On Dennett.* Belmont, CA: Wadsworth.

Zawidzki, Tadeusz (2007), *Dennett.* Oxford: Oneworld Publications.

INTELLECTUAL AUTOBIOGRAPHIES OF DENNETT

Dennett, Daniel C. (1994), "Self-Portrait," in Guttenplan, S., ed., *A Companion to the Philosophy of Mind.* Oxford: Blackwell, pp. 236–244. Reprinted in BC, pp. 355–366.

Dennett, Daniel C. "Daniel Dennett Autobiography Part 1," *Philosophy Now*, Jul/Aug 2008 Issue 68, pp. 22–26.

Dennett, Daniel C. "Daniel Dennett Autobiography Part 2," *Philosophy Now*, Sep/Oct 2008 Issue 69, pp. 21–25.

INDEX

Boldfaced references indicate either a definition or a passage that focuses themat-
ically on the issue

Archimedean perch 88
Archimedean stand 147
Aristotelian forms 12, 63, 67
Aristotle 63, 65, 67, 71–2, 149
arms race 125, 130
ASCII code 21, 47
atheism(-ists) 139, 143
atomic experiences 12, 39
  impressions 37
  intuitions 12
atoms 85, 90, 93, 103
attribution 5, 35, 82, 85–7, **95–7**
  of action 82, 85
  of belief **89–96**, 100, 136, 141, 150
  and context 94–6, 155
  of experience 84
  global 18–19, 25, 52, 85, 86, 96
  of intentionality 70, 96–7
  of meaning 154–5
  of responsibility 52, 81, 107
  self-attribution 85
  and stance 91, 93–5, 102, 105, 107, 155
  value-laden 96
author 15–16, 84
  of record 86
authority, absolute or privileged 15–16, 55
autobiography 84
automaton 79
  see also robot; Shakey the robot
autophenomenology 14
autostimulation 51
avoidable **114–15**, 118
  see also inevitability

Baron d'Holbach 4, 13
bats 38
battle of New Orleans 30
beaver's dam 79–80
beetle in the box 141
behavior 43–4
  information-sensitive 118
  "internal" 46
behaviorism(-ist) 2, 5, 35, 44, 96
  abhorred by Dennett 96
beings-in-themselves 148
  see also things-in-themselves

belief 22, 39, 41, 44–5, 91, 100, 101, 103
  avow (profess) belief 131, 132, 140–1
  belief in belief 139–41, 144
  and cause 101
  content left to experts 140
  and desire 40, 52, **90–3**, 95, 97, 100, 136
  environment 121
  and functions 97
  in God 132, 139
  intentional-level concept 97–8
  invisible from design stance 92
  paradoxical 141
  propositional 94
  reality of **92–8**
  religious 132, 136, 139, 144, 145
  right to 144
  second-order 138–40
  specification of 94, 98, 100
  of thermostats 91, 96–7
  without content 140
  see also attribution, of belief; cats eat fish
believers 132, 136, 139, 142
benselfishness 124–5, 127
Berkeley, George 89
billiards 109
biological evolution 74, 76, 118
  see also adaptation; Darwinian; evolution
biological necessity 67
biological possibility 66
biological survival 127–8, 130
biology 63, 118–19, 148–9
  laws of (regularities) 4, 66–7
bitmap 21, 99
black-and-white thinking 68, 70, 98, 112
  see also all-or-nothing
blame 18
blindsight 36, **42–3**
bluff 125
body 13, 19, 44, 78, 85, 86, 154
  death of 86
  representation of 80–1
bogus concept 104
bogus memory 28
Boss neuron 86
bowerbird 135